A HAUNTED SOUL

A TRUE STORY OF ONE MAN'S STRUGGLE WITH THE PARANORMAL

BY

JASON DOWD

AND

JOHN GREENBURG

Model on the Cover – Charlene Amis
https://www.facebook.com/profile.php?id=1830327675

Models Pictured in "Dreams, Nightmares, Fears and Fantasy" Vol 1 series
Charlene Amis – Demon vs. Angel
Brian Amis – Demon vs. Angel
Faythe Monbleau – Trapped but not Dead
Willow Marcotte – Death to Yesterday

Dedication

First and foremost, I dedicate this book and my abilities to my Lord and Savior who has given me such wonderful gifts and made me a strong individual. I only hope my stories and my art open the eyes of those who do not believe to Your everlasting love and mercy.

I also want to thank my family, who instilled the amazing values I have today. You showed me love, without judging me, after I told you the entire story of my life… even the things you were unaware of. This was something I was afraid to do because I never wanted you to think of me in a bad light. To me, that would have been a fate worse than death. I love you all so very much that you can't imagine how much.

Next, I want to thank my wife Fran for putting up with my crazy life. I know it's not easy living with me. In fact it's hard for ME to live with me (LOL), but you do it with grace, kindness and a heart that's larger than the planets above. Your beauty and your smile melt away the craziness that is my life and make me thankful to have found such an amazing person to call my wife and best friend. You can't imagine how much I love you. You know this story is really just beginning. I'm sure we will witness many more chapters unfold before us!

I also want to say "Thank you" to my friends. Some of you have known about some of the stuff contained in this book. To those of you who didn't, I hope this explains a little bit more about me. I realize how important friendship is. Friendship is something I will never again take for granted. Having you in my life… and you know who you are… makes the world a better place.

In addition, I want to say "Thank you" to Kim and Mike Rebman. I have enjoyed the ghost hunting adventures we have been on together. You are like a brother and sister to me. Your friendship means so much to us. I can't imagine my life without you. Thank you so much for making us the godparents of Bella… that was one of the nicest things anyone could have given us. You should know that… as long as I am living and breathing… your children will always have a home and unconditional love. And the same goes for you, as well.

I want to say "Thank you" to John Greenburg, the co-author of this book. You helped me put into words what I have been trying to express for years. I can't thank you enough, and I hope that you have learned something along the way. Thanks for being a friend!

I also dedicate this book to the loving memory of Velma (Miller) Smith aka "Ama" (my grandmother I felt so close to) (1920-1999), Robert E. Dowd (my grandpa) (1919-1995), Thomas Gillooly (my great grandpa) (1895-1993), Mary Gillooly (my great grandmother) (1900-1986), Imelda Dowd aka "Nana" (my grandmother) (1920-1980), Adela Miller aka "Tantie" (my great aunt) (1913-2005) and all my other family members who have passed away. I miss you all very much and hope to someday see you again in Heaven. I also dedicate this book to Paul Knox (1979 – 2006). You are my best friend and will always be. I wish I could have told you in person. You told me after your death that I should write a book, so here it is buddy!

I also dedicate this book to the Knox family, Nellie, Carolyn, Leanne and David; who in my eyes are MY family as well. I love you all very much. I hate that you had to experience so much loss… but look how strong you are! You're my inspiration.

P.S.: I don't remember which of you wanted me to be an author and which of you wanted me to be an artist, but I just want to say to Ama and Mom: You both have your wish! I promised you I would be both an artist and an author, and I never gave up on keeping that promise.

Introduction

For as long as I can remember, people have looked at my art work and have often asked me: "What goes on in your head?" It is hard for me to give them a brief explanation. My art says a lot, but to understand the art, you have to understand me.

This book is an account of my life, and all of the stories are true. It will show you how I dealt with bullies, the paranormal and my recently accepted psychic abilities. What I once thought made me strange and what I tried to hide, I now realize makes me special and sets me apart from the crowd.

I have many quirks in my life. I am a strange individual who endured a lot growing up. Those events and experiences… both good and bad… have made me who I am today. I became a strong-willed, open-minded person with a lot of self-control. I hope my story inspires others who may be going through things similar to what I did and helps them to realize they will be okay, after all.

I want my story to show people that it's wonderful to be different. If you don't blend in with everyone else, it's probably because you were made to stand out. I want people to realize that when it comes to the paranormal, it's okay to talk to people about it. Some will believe you and some won't, but regardless, it's there around us and we must accept it and deal with it. Who knows? You might tell your story to someone and find out that they feel the same way you do, and they just might tell you their story in return. There is also the possibility that the communication between you and the other person could kindle a friendship… and that would be the best thing of all.

The most important thing overall I would like you to understand is that you must be true to who you are and never let anyone dictate your life or try to change you. I was fortunate to have realized that my entire life. Some accepted me and some didn't. Those who didn't probably missed out on having a wonderful friendship.

I also want to encourage anyone with a story of the paranormal to please talk to me. I am here to listen and help you get to the bottom of your trouble. Not everything that happens to you is a case of the paranormal or a ghost. Don't be fooled by my background… I approach the paranormal with a scientific point of view. Using my psychic ability, I can lend a sixth sense to find out if you have a spirit or not… the scientific evidence solidifies what I already know.

You can e-mail me any time at: sales@dowdstudios.com and share your evidence. I will be glad to look it over.

Chapter 1 – Understanding Me

I have been in a struggle with the paranormal my entire life. In order to fully understand the incidents I am about to relate, it is vitally important for you to grasp who I am and what I believe in. You will find my story entertaining, but it is also intended to be indicative of life-changing implications and struggles.

Since birth, my life seems to have a "Yin Yang" quality to it. By "Yin Yang", I am referring to the ancient Chinese belief that there are two complementary forces in the universe. One is Yin, which represents everything negative or feminine. The other is Yang, which represents everything good or masculine. It is important to understand, that one is not better than the other. What is bad for some people is very good for other people. I have led a "Yin Yang" life in the sense that my life seems to have followed a pattern in which there has always been an unexpected, completely opposite situation awaiting me around the corner.

For instance, my mother's attending physician predicted that I would be born on Halloween. As far as she was concerned, this was not good news. My mom came from a staunch Lutheran background, and she would not allow that to happen if she could possibly help it. Unfortunately for her, she went into labor with me on Halloween… just as her doctor had predicted. I don't know how she did it, but she got her wish. I was born on November 1st, 1978 at one minute before noon. So, rather than being born on what Mom considered a pagan holiday and the evilest day of the year, I somehow wound up being birthed on All Saints' Day, which is probably the third holiest day on the calendar.

If that doesn't get you wondering then maybe this will. I was born in Connecticut, where it would usually be snowing on the first day of November. On the day I was born, though, it was pouring rain outside and it turned out to be much warmer than expected, but it was also one of the dreariest days they had all year. On the day of my baptism, however, which is a symbol of new birth in the Christian faith, there happened to be a blanket of snow on the ground... in the form of frozen rain. It was the complete opposite of the weather in which I was born.

These are just two examples of my Yin Yang life. I could go on and name more, but that would be redundant. The point that I'm trying to make is that events which took place at the beginning of my life painted a picture of how my life would play out in the future.

There have been many times throughout my existence when I just happened to be at places around the nation just as something unusual was taking place and in each instance, this happened totally by accident. These were places where either great tragedies or joyous jubilations occurred.

An example of this occurred in July, 1996, when I went to visit my grandparents in Connecticut. Nothing odd happened during the entire trip until the night before I was to fly back to Florida. The tranquility was rudely interrupted by a sonic boom rippling through the air, almost as if a space shuttle had breached the atmosphere on its descent back to Earth. Both my grandmother and I wondered what it was. I later found out that it was the sound of TWA Flight 800 that went down over the Long Island coast. The next day, security was extra tight at Bradley International Airport, and my flight was delayed for a few hours, all because of the tragedy.

Almost one year to the day, in July, 1997, my father and I went to Miami to see a Florida Marlins major league baseball game. While we were in town, we decided to take a spin down Ocean Drive in the South Beach area. I stopped to take pictures of a visually attractive multi-million dollar mansion, only to find out later that day Gianni Versace, a famous fashion designer who is acknowledged as creating the "supermodel", was murdered in that very residence by spree killer Andrew Cunanan. In fact Versace's body had been moved just two hours before we arrived at his house. Of course we were totally unaware at the time that a famous designer had been murdered, and that we were standing at the scene of his demise. What made matters even stranger was that we happened to be staying at a hotel which was only three miles from the house boat that Cunanan occupied while he was on the run. The house boat was also the place where the killer took his own life.

Earlier that same year, right after my high school graduation, my dear friend Shawn and I went to Texas to attend a gymnastics competition in Fort Worth. While we were there, we decided to drive to Oklahoma, since we weren't too far away. We happened to arrive in Oklahoma City just as the remains of the Alfred P. Murrah Federal Building had been leveled. The building had been destroyed in the infamous Oklahoma City bombing which occurred in April, 1995… the most destructive act of terrorism on American shores until the September 11, 2001 attacks. The bombing claimed 168 lives, including 19 children under the age of six. The ruins of the building were being replaced by a memorial to the victims.

In 2002, my wife Frances and I decided to go on a four-day, three-city tour to watch major league baseball games. We planned to stop in Baltimore for an Orioles game, in Philadelphia for a Phillies game and in New York for a Yankees game. On our last stop, which was Yankee Stadium, we went sightseeing through Manhattan to pass the time away before the first pitch of the game we would be attending. We happened to be at Ground Zero just a few hours shy of watching the last girder leave the site of the 9/11 terrorist attacks. I ended up taking pictures of that historical event.

Earlier that same year, in March, 2002, Frances and I decided to go on a sightseeing trip to Texas with my friend Shawn. Along the way, we decided to make a stop in San Antonio and see the Alamo. Upon arriving, we parked in front of a glass enclosed indoor shopping plaza that was adjacent to the landmark. We parked our car and planned to get out when we heard what sounded like a bomb going off.

Our instinctive response was to panic, since we could actually see the glass walls of the indoor mall vibrate. This was a knee jerk reaction, since it had only been a few months after the September 11th attacks. We hurried out of the car and went to investigate, hoping that one of America's landmarks was still intact. To our surprise, we discovered that what we had heard were the sounds of an annual reenactment of the Battle of the Alamo. The reenactment was not any casual affair; it was a highly organized, well-staged hour and a half battle that featured hundreds of participants firing off black powder, pistols and cannons.

These are just a few examples of the many times I have witnessed a tragic incident, been within close proximity of a tragic incident at the time it occurred, been to the site of where a tragedy had recently occurred or have been present for a joyous celebration. At this point, you're probably asking: "What does all of that prove?'

It proves that I have led an interesting life and have a history of strange things happening to me. So far, the first three decades of my time on earth have been a "Yin Yang life"… I have shown a pattern of being in the right place at the right time to be a part of history. And at the age of 33, I'm sure there is much more to come.

Chapter 2 - My Religion

The next part of my life you will need to understand is my religion and my beliefs. By understanding these things you will become aware of the intense internal battle I have to live with each and every day. In the past, this pressure was intensified by the threat of rejection from my family and those who knew me if I dared tell anyone about the paranormal things that happened to me.

From the moment of my birth, religion has been a huge factor in my life. My father was a Roman Catholic, but not a practicing one. When he was growing up, he never missed Mass because his mother (my paternal grandmother) made sure he went. He went to a Catholic boarding school, attended Mass regularly and was a frequent communicant. That changed, however, after he graduated from high school.

My mother was raised in the Missouri Synod Lutheran faith. It is the second strictest denomination of Lutherans. Both of my maternal grandparents, as well as the rest of my family on that side, were active, practicing Lutherans. My Grandpa remains so to this day… and he is 89 going on 90. My maternal grandfather's parents were charter members of a Lutheran church in Terryville, Connecticut, while my maternal grandmother's parents were charter members of Immanuel Lutheran Church in Bristol. This is the very same church where my mother, my aunt and uncle were baptized and my mother was married to my father.

Immanuel Lutheran was the church where I was baptized. I also attended that church's elementary school, following in the tradition of my mother.

Since my dad was not a practicing Catholic, Mom and Dad both decided to raise me as a Lutheran, like my mother. This pleased my mom's parents but caused a huge problem within my dad's family.

My great grandfather on my dad's side was very disappointed that I would be raised Lutheran, but he loved me just the same; and I loved him. Because of this decision made by my parents, though, I barely even saw the rest of my dad's family, with the exception of my great grandfather. My paternal grandmother, whom I called "Nana", died before my brother was born, and I was only two years old at the time; so I hardly knew her. Needless to say, religious differences caused a rift in my extended family and because of that, I hardly know my dad's side of my family tree.

I attended Immanuel Lutheran School for grades one through six. It was a very strict school, similar to Catholic schools. One hour of each school day was set aside for religious instruction. I memorized Dr. Martin Luther's Large Catechism (also referred to as The Book of Concord) before I reached third grade, and I attended church every Wednesday. That was in addition to my parents taking us to church every Sunday. In some cases, such as Lent, we also attended church every Thursday and Saturday. As a result, during my formative years, I practically lived at church and I lived by what I was taught.

In terms of beliefs, the Lutherans believe in the Doctrine of the Triune God… meaning God the Father, God the Son (Jesus) and God the Holy Spirit. They also believe that these entities are separate people, yet one God. God gave his only son, Jesus Christ, to come to Earth and to die for our sins. His blood washed the way the sins of the world and in his resurrection, we shall forever sustain eternal life; if we believe He died for our sins and was resurrected on the third day.

Unlike the Catholics, the Lutherans do not pray to saints or to the Virgin Mary. They believe that the saints and the Blessed Mother are important figures in theology, but they have no power to heal or save. When the Lutherans pray, they pray in the name of Jesus Christ, because the Bible states: "Jesus said: 'Anyone who wants to come to the Father, must come through Me.'"

They also believe that you can't get to Heaven on good deeds. Good deeds are things that should be done by everyone, everyday. Lutherans believe it takes more to get to Heaven than good deeds alone. They believe that to accomplish this task, you must accept that Jesus died for you.

In addition, Lutherans believe that when you die, you are dead. You will be judged before the almighty God and you will either be cast into Hell or live in peace and harmony in Heaven with Him. They do not believe in Purgatory, or in reincarnation. They believe you have one chance at life to live as God would want you to live and that upon death, you will judged by the Lord. If you have any unfinished business, then it will remain unfinished; because your spirit will not be able to communicate with the living.

The concepts of "ghosts" or "hauntings" do not fit at all into the Lutheran equation. Whenever there are reports of hauntings, the Lutheran church tends to claim any haunting as being a possible demonic or non-human haunting. In response, they will usually offer prayers and a blessing of the home involved. As far as the leaders of that denomination are concerned, when you are dead, you are dead and cannot come back or have any contact with the living. They do believe in demons, though, because the Bible states demons exist. You must bear in mind, however, that to Lutherans, demons are non-human entities.

I was taught in my Lutheran religious instruction that anyone for any reason can be saved and spared from a life of eternal death in Hell at any time; even in their last minutes on earth. In order to be saved, they must repent of their sins, ask God for true forgiveness and accept Jesus Christ as their Lord and Savior. In so doing, according to the Bible, God will forgive their sins and take them into his arms, regardless what they did on earth.

The fact that the Apostle Paul was once a vicious murderer and Christian persecutor named Saul is a true testament to this very claim. He became one of Jesus' most trusted apostles, and he wrote a good portion of the Holy Bible. From what I was taught, there is no question that God forgave Paul and embraced him. This can also be stated based on the criminal hanging on the cross next to Jesus, who said: "Jesus, Remember me when you enter the Kingdom of Heaven" and Jesus responded: "Today, you will be with Me in paradise."

This is what I was taught all through school and throughout my formative years. In April of 1993, I was confirmed in the Lutheran faith, meaning that I professed to the church that I accepted the teachings and beliefs my parents had chosen for me at baptism. I also professed that I believed the Lutheran doctrine to be true and, without doubt, the true representation of Christ and the one true path to eternal life.

Today, I still believe in the Lutheran doctrine and its teachings. This is what makes the incidents which I will relate in this story the cause of such conflict within me. I have never doubted my religion, but now I find myself unable to prove that my religion is providing all the answers which are needed. If the teachings of Lutheranism are true, then what I have experienced should never have happened… and I know that they happened because I lived through them.

Chapter 3 - My Fears and My Upbringing

Every kid deserves a childhood. The childhood years are necessary for any human being to become emotionally and psychologically centered. For reasons beyond my control, I was denied a happy, innocent childhood.

I was born in Bristol, Connecticut. For those who might not know, Connecticut is part of an area that is very old. Some of the towns existed even before Connecticut was a colony, let alone a state. Connecticut has towns that were founded in 1630's and in some cases, even earlier.

This long, rich history also makes the area very susceptible to being haunted. For instance, the house I lived in when I was a new born infant was located on the George Washington Turnpike in Burlington. This was the route General George Washington followed when he led his army on its southward trek towards New York. While he was in Connecticut, he was ambushed by Indians who had aligned with the British. Washington and his men were able to emerge victorious, and they continued along their route. With the many Revolutionary War casualties spread across the landscape, as well as deaths from battles with the British in 1812 and skirmishes with local Indian tribes spanning 200 years, the area was full of murder and untimely death.

There was history everywhere I turned in Connecticut. I remember going to the "cross" on Willis Street, which was one street over from the road in Bristol where my maternal grandfather lived. Grandpa and I liked to walk through the woods just for fun. I particularly remember this one particular walk we had one Friday night.

As we walked through the woods we stumbled upon an abandoned graveyard that was in total disarray. The grass was taller than the head stones and in some cases; trees grew right through some of the stone markings. It was a creepy site, but something that was not uncommon in Connecticut and the other New England states. After looking around at the headstones, we noticed that most of the burials had taken place between 1730 and 1790. A few markers were in the early 19th century, but none were dated later than 1830.

Scenes like this can easily cause a haunting… a "residual haunting" in most cases, but nonetheless a haunting. Another factor is that Connecticut is rich in quartz, a mineral most watches use as a power source. Quartz rocks are able to trap energy and release it. Since humans are made of energy, and time itself is a form of energy, it's possible that places where the ground is rich in quartz can capture that energy and play it back almost like a film projector… and this would result in a residual haunting.

To sum it up, I grew up hearing all kinds of ghost stories and was told of places in and around my state where hauntings were alleged to have taken place… and Connecticut is filled with them. As proof, you only need to watch the reality series *Ghost Hunters* on the SyFy cable TV channel… just about every other investigation takes place in my old home state.

Hearing about all these hauntings while I was growing up made me horrified at the idea of death. It caused such trauma for me that I would even experience panic attacks if I went to cemeteries.

This fear was heightened by the first wake I ever attended, which was for my great grandmother on my dad's side. Seeing her there in her casket, looking like a wax figure, seemed so disturbingly surreal to me. I was horrified at what I saw. It was hard for me to comprehend that she would never move again; and that she was to be buried six feet underground, never again being able to reach the surface of the earth. That thought just scared me to death. I couldn't imagine myself in her situation, but in knowing death was inevitable, I knew that someday I would find myself in that very same situation. As a result, I developed a fear of being buried.

That fear still affects me today. My wife Frances knows that I don't ever want to be buried underground. I insist that I be buried with all my blood and organs, and buried with a crowbar in my coffin. And my coffin must be placed in a mausoleum or crypt.

When I first became aware of this fear, I thought that there was something terribly wrong with me. I was ashamed of it and I wouldn't talk about it to anyone. Only recently I have learned that fear of being buried prematurely is fairly common, and that I am not the only one with such a fear. The reason so little is said about it is that many people who suffer from it are too ashamed to talk about it.

The task of defeating my fear was no cake walk, but I finally managed to face my fear head on. This victory would transpire during my 8th grade year in a way that had two horrific downsides. The first was that I was subjected to gruesome images. The second was that it also challenged everything that I had been taught, that I knew and that I believed to be true.

So now that you know about the inner sanctum of my life, the rest of this story should come together for you. I hope it will help you understand the vicious conflicts I have in life, conflicts which made the triumph over these fears that much sweeter.

Some of the stories I am about to relate are short, but I have tried to keep them in chronological order. In the end, if you have followed along, I hope that you feel the same jubilation I did later in life. You will see how I gained my courage to take on these challenges and how important your history and upbringing can be to your future.

I would also like every person who was deprived of their childhood to realize that they are not alone and that their life can get better for them. They have nothing to be ashamed of, because what happened to them was not their fault. Problems are solved through human to human contact, building lines of meaningful communication and sharing concerns for each other's problems.

Chapter 4 – My First Reoccurring Dream

Have you ever experienced a dream that seems to come back again and again, night after night, throughout your life? I never could understand how that happens or why, but it has happened to me.

My first reoccurring dream was horrifying, especially since it started when I was six years old. It took me 26 years to figure out the meaning, and when I finally did, the nightmare vanished. I would have this dream anywhere from one and two times a year, but sometimes as frequently as three times in one week.

The dream only added to my horror with death. It was something no six-year-old child should be able to comprehend, let alone know the workings of. I always kept it to myself because I didn't want my parents to think I was nuts, and when you hear what my dream was, you will understand why I was so unwilling to talk about it.

As I have said, I began having this dream when I was six years old. I would always wake up in a cold sweat every time I experienced it. The dream never changed; it was the same every time. It only intensified in the sensual aspects. As time went by, the smells, the sounds, the feelings grew stronger and stronger and each time I had the dream, I felt as though I were living it in real life.

By the time I was nine, I started to wonder if somehow I had actually lived what I was dreaming. It was so vivid and real that I had a hard time deciding whether or not it was a dream.

My Dream of Being Buried Alive

The nightmare would always start with my waking up in a casket. I am startled by the sound of dirt being thrown in my lonely grave. The dirt makes a loud thud, followed by a rustling sound as it rolls off the aluminum lid of my casket. I try to see where I am, but the darkness is so black that even a flame cannot penetrate it.

I try to reach out with my arms, but the box I'm confined in is so tight that I can barely move my arms from my side. The top of the lid is just inches from my face, and the fear of claustrophobia starts to set in.

As the dirt fills up over the coffin, I start to hear the sound of the dirt become more and more faint. Soon, I no longer hear the sound of dirt being thrown on me. I begin to wonder if they have finished filling the grave in.

With all the dirt surrounding my box of rest, the silence becomes eerily stagnant. It is an unusual and uneasy quiet, and the silk lining of my casket insulates the sound even more. I start to panic because I want to sit up, but I can't, since the lid of the casket is only inches from my head.

I scream for help, begging those above to get me out of here because I am alive. Sadly, my efforts are futile; they cannot hear me.

I pound on the sides of the casket, only to hurt my hands; so I decide to claw my way out, giving hope to one last effort of escape. That fails, and the lining of the casket soon lies in shreds on my belly. I begin to panic even worse until tears roll down my face. I see my own mortality start to set in. My life passes before my eyes, and the worst part of it is that I know what my casket will be like because I am in it.

The casket becomes cold because of the moist dirt all around it. The weight of the soil starts to cave the lid in.

It's getting harder to breathe because I have used up more than half of the oxygen and the area is being filled with carbon dioxide. I can actually smell the moisture of the ground around me, and the moisture starts to cause condensation on the inner panels of the casket.

Breathing becomes nearly impossible. I start to see stars and I feel very weak and faint. I start to hallucinate while insanity begins to set in, causing me to laugh without any reason. I take my last breath. The last thing I see is the ripped lining of my casket… which represents my last hope of survival. I then look down on my final resting place, a view I should never have seen if I were alive.

That was my dream, and that is still the reason I do not want to be buried when I die. It is also the reason that I distrust doctors. Because of this dream, I don't ever want an autopsy upon my death. I want to be buried with all my blood and organs as intact as when I died. The reason for this is that once an autopsy is performed, if the doctors are wrong and you were not dead, they have now killed you for real. For me, an autopsy is an invasion of my privacy and is against my religious beliefs.

I'm sure you can understand that it is not acceptable for a six-year-old to have intimate knowledge of what death is like… or to experience a dream like mine. As I grew older, I felt as though I had interacted with people who had lived in the past, but according to my religion, that was impossible. So if it is impossible to have any sort of experience with a past life, what other explanation could there be? If I had a dream this vivid, it would almost suggest that I had lived it. How else could a child be that specific and have so much detail in their dream?

I first had this dream in 1984, two years before I went to the wake for my great grandmother. When I saw her lying in her casket, I had a major case of *de ja vu*… a flashback which brought back the vivid images and smells from my haunting dream. I truly believed I knew what she was in for. Luckily for her, she was dead when she had been placed in her coffin and never experienced the horror I did in my dream.

Even though I have confronted my fear, I still get flashbacks every time I see a dead person. Despite my ability to overcome the fear, I still experience the smells and sounds.

I don't like funerals, but really, who does? My dislike is even more intense, though, because of how vivid my memories of my dream are. Flashbacks of those sights and smells can still send me into an immediate panic attack. I have coped with this by somehow learning to hide my panic attacks from those around me. As time has gone by, I have learned to mask them well.

I never told anyone about this dream before, because they would say I was crazy. I didn't want to be burdened with that label, so I kept it to myself and faced the realism of my own mortality from age six.

I wasn't able to get over my fear of death until 2009. I was able to do it by embracing my religion which gave me comfort. I know that I will die someday, but I will be at the side of my Lord and Savior when that day comes, living in eternal life.

The dream continued to surface in my sleep till I was 31 years old. In 2010, I managed to stop the dream for good by capturing it on film. I produced a series of photos which is part of my *Dreams, Nightmares, Fears and Fantasy Collection: Volume One*.

The series of photos tells the story. A young child lies in a casket, having been certified as dead by the doctors; only she isn't dead. She wakes up in a panic, trying to escape the death trap she has found herself in. She claws at the casket, but can't escape. Finally she dies, and only then is she truly free.

At the time I was working on the project, I didn't realize why I chose to portray a girl in my photo series *Trapped, But Not Dead.* Subconsciously, I was using the pictures to tell the story of the nightmare I had endured for years. It finally all made sense to me in 2010 when a life-altering revelation was finally made known to me.

dowdstudios

dowdstudios

dowelstudios

dowdstudios

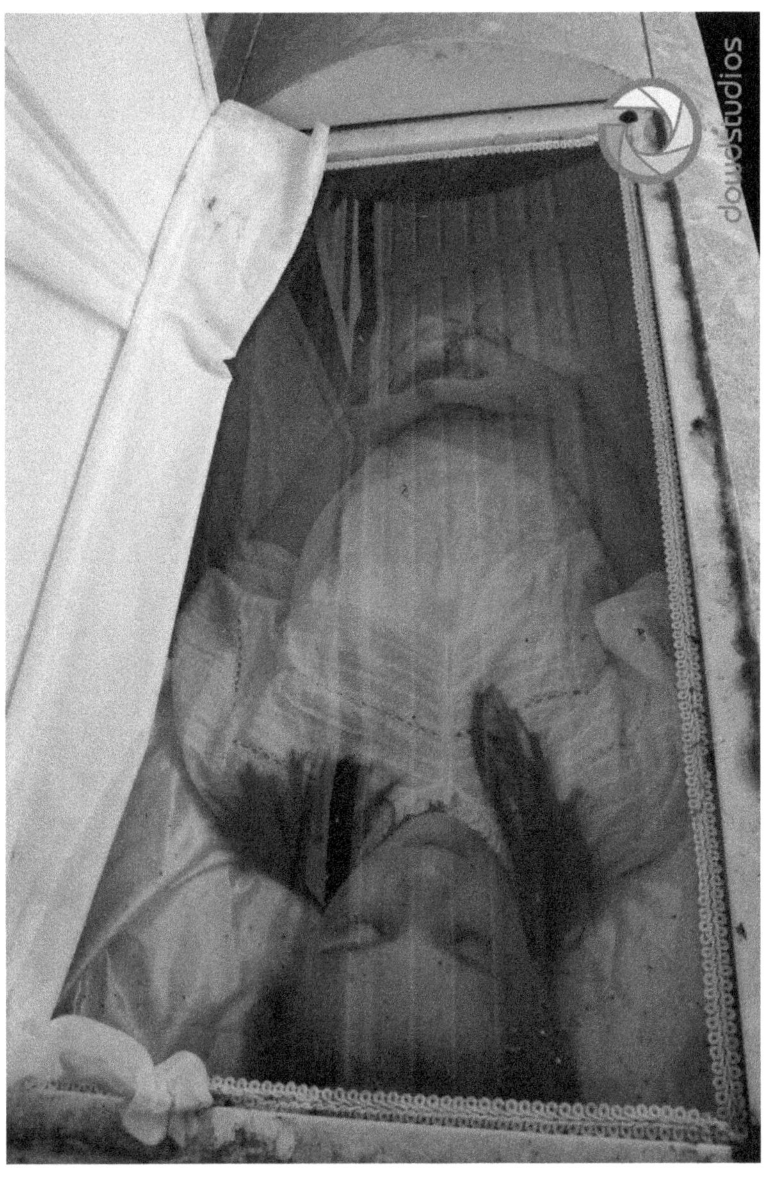

31

Chapter 5 – The Green Lady

Have you ever seen a ghost? I have. I have actually seen them quite often, and I still do to this very day. Sometimes I think I am a magnet for the deceased… why, I have no idea. All I can say is this: "The ability to see the dead is quite unique and awesome, but unless your constitution allows you to handle this, it can be quite disturbing."

For a long time, I thought it was a curse; but now I see it as a blessing. I was always considered an outsider growing up. I knew I was a bit strange and for that very reason I didn't want anyone to know I was able to see ghosts. It was difficult enough for me to be even remotely popular. You can imagine what would have happened if I had told people I could see ghosts. I would have been forever ridiculed, even though it was the damn truth.

I possessed a certain power during the time I was growing up, and still do today; it started at a very young age. If I could get near somebody… if I could touch them or have someone give a good description of them… I was able to feel their emotions and I could see vivid images of incidents in their life. I could also tell if someone was lying or if they were a bad person based on my impressions of them. I call these impressions "energy readings".

Those who know me will be quick to tell you that I generally keep my distance from people, and there is a reason for that. It's not that I am being rude, or meaning to come off that way. My gift is very intense and there is great power in my visions and emotions. For those reasons, I really don't want to know that much about anyone. When I was a kid, all this meant was that I was "Mr. Unpopular".

I didn't know if the people around me could see the ghosts too, so I always kept my distance. There were only certain people that I allowed to come over to my home and hang out with me. I never went to parties and I never went over to friends' houses that much.

If the spirits were following me, I didn't want anyone to get startled and/or horrified over what they saw, if they could see them. Could you imagine if the few people I knew could see what might be following me? I wouldn't have had any friends at all. I couldn't just say: "Wow, dude, did you see that?"

It took me some time before I realized that nobody else could see what I was seeing. If I asked anyone if they happened to see what I saw, the reply I usually got was something like: "See what?" If you hear that enough times, you will start to question your own sanity.

So, I went through my entire childhood holding this secret inside. I was very secretive about the fact that I could see the spirits of dead people and that I didn't want to touch people because I could absorb their emotions, as well as incidents that hurt them or made them happy.

When I think back on it all, I can tell you the exact moment I saw my first ghost. Since I was just a kid, I said something about it and I was quickly silenced and reminded about my religious beliefs. I let the matter drop, but I went six more years knowing I saw a ghost and that I would need some kind of evidence to prove it. Good luck on that one.

Let me tell you about that fateful day, er… night. It was Halloween, 1987; the eve of my ninth birthday. School had just let out at Immanuel Lutheran, and I was on my way to meet my grandfather. He picked me up at school every night and drove me home to Southington. That night was special because it was a Friday. This meant I was going to my grandparents' house for dinner, and then they would bring me home around 7:00 P.M.

Back in 1987, I loved watching the Nickelodeon channel on cable TV. Unfortunately, the cable system in Southington, where I lived, had not picked up Nickelodeon yet. So, the only way I could watch such shows as *You Can't Do That On Television,*

Mysterious Cities of Gold, Turkey Television and *Dennis the Menace* was at my grandparents home in Bristol. It was my Friday treat.

The Friday night in question was even more special because it was Halloween and I would probably go out trick-or-treating when I arrived home. It was also possible that my grandfather might even take me out to do something before taking me to my house. He liked doing things with me on Fridays, and it was something I also enjoyed.

While I was still walking through the school hallway, I put on a knitted cap my grandmother had made for me. The temperature was in the low 40's, with crisp New England breezes making it quite cold outside. I put on my jacket, threw my backpack over my shoulder and ran out the front door of the school.

As soon as the crisp New England chill hit my cheeks, they turned beet red, but I didn't care. This time however I didn't see my grandfather's car sitting there ready to take me home. I saw my father's car. Dad was going to pick me up instead.

I opened the door to his car. He put down the book he had been reading patted me on my shoulder. "Hi Jason," he said as I buckled up.

I replied: "Hi Dad, why are you picking me up today?"

He said: "Well your grandfather isn't feeling well and since we are going trick or treating tonight I thought I would pick you up. I can bring you by to see Ama and Grandpa before going home. She has some goodies for you." Every time I visited her, she would give me a bag of assorted cookies and a stick of gum.

He continued by saying: "Then, I'm to take you home to get you ready for trick-or-treating."

Honestly, I was a little disappointed that I would be going home rather than spending time with my grandparents and watching Nickelodeon like I usually did on Friday nights, but I understood.

I also enjoyed spending time with my Dad. We always did some cool things together.

As we drove to their home, my dad said: "Maybe we can still do something. Maybe we can go to the Green Lady Cemetery."

I thought that was so cool! Despite my fear of death, Connecticut cemeteries were the best! I loved the old headstones with the angel faces carved in, along with the look and feel of the stones. Plus, it was fun to see how long ago it was when the people buried there passed away.

I had been to the "Green Lady Cemetery" before. It was a very haunted cemetery… or so I had been told. I had never actually seen anything strange take place there, but the old burial place did have an odd feel to it. I was never really sure if all the talk about the Green Lady Cemetery was just my father and my uncle's way of playing tricks on me to scare me, but I never had any proof that what they were saying wasn't true either.

I was always excited to go to that cemetery because most of the inhabitants had died during the War of 1812, and some even earlier in the 1790s. It was amazing to see graves that old.

I have always felt a connection to the Green Lady Cemetery because it is on an elevation near Chippen's Hill and at one time, my great grandfather on my mother's side owned just about that whole mountain. My great grandfather was a first generation immigrant from Germany. He owned this farm house in Bristol, Connecticut, which a historic house that was a bed and breakfast back in the 1700's. There is talk George Washington may have stayed there. I also felt a connection to that cemetery because I had lived right around the corner from it before we moved to Southington when I was a year old.

Sometimes I would go to that cemetery to get "gravestone rubbings"; sometimes we would just go to admire the beautiful landscape surrounding this place of history and mystique. Sometimes my dad would take me hunting for antique bottles at the old foundation behind the cemetery. It was alleged to be the foundation upon which the home of "Elizabeth" was built, and Elizabeth was allegedly the lady who haunted the cemetery.

After my Dad suggested we go to that cemetery on that particular occasion, I couldn't say no. I was excited and nervous knowing that it was Halloween. If anything would happen, tonight would be the night.

Just as soon as I picked up my goodies from Ama, we would be off to Burlington to see the cemetery. When we pulled up to Grandpa's house, I jumped out of the car, ran into the basement and then pounded up the steps to the kitchen where my grandmother was cooking. I ran to her and gave her a huge hug as I always did. She kissed my head and brought me to the dining room table.

We talked about school, how my week had been and what sort of costume I would wear. As I recall, I went trick or treating as Garfield, the cartoon cat, that year.

Then, my dad came up the stairs to the kitchen and told Ama that he was going to take me to The Green Lady. Oh boy, did my grandmother get mad!!

Ama said my dad would have to explain to my mom why I was late, and he agreed to accept all the blame.

Now we were ready to go. My grandmother gave me my bag of cookies. Then she checked my hat to make sure it covered my ears, gave me a huge hug and kiss and sent me back to the car with Dad.

I could always tell when we got close to the cemetery because it gave off this odd vibe. It was about 4:30 P.M. when we got there… and it was pitch black outside. You have to take into account that it gets darker earlier up north because Connecticut extends farther past the Atlantic coast line than a place like Miami, Florida.

We pulled up next to the cemetery. Its perimeter was defined by an old colonial stone wall that had been built back in the 1700's.

At that time it had a wrought iron fence built on top of the wall. It looked just like the ones you see in fairy tale books surrounding Victorian houses that allegedly have witches living there. That probably added more uneasiness to the mystique of the location.

When I got out of the car, it was so cold I could see my breath. My hands grew white and my nose turned red from the cold. I wasted no time running straight to the entrance. I was ready to go in.

Perhaps the oddest thing about the place was that when I walked in past the outer wall, I immediately experienced a dizzy feeling, almost like I had stood on my head and then quickly became upright. A blood rush would be the most accurate way of describing that feeling.

We didn't stay long because it was getting late and my dad already had a lot of explaining to do with my mom when he finally got me home. We pretty much just walked around, looked at the stones and speculated about the cause of death of each departed person we walked past. It was a lot of fun, I must admit. I personally think most of them died from some kind of pandemic, such as yellow fever, because so many had died in the same month of the same year. There were also soldiers from the Revolutionary War and the War of 1812 buried there.

When Dad told me it was getting late and we needed to go, the place suddenly grew very eerie. Little hairs on the back of my neck stood up, and I think the hair on my head did too… at least that's what it felt like.

I ran to the car. My dad was moving slower, but he eventually caught up with me. He had locked the car, so I had to wait for him to get to the car so I could get in. My blood rush feeling was gone, the moon was high in the sky, but the creepy feeling had not subsided; in fact it had intensified.

As my dad fumbled with his keys, I took another look at the cemetery. The moonlight lit up the burial ground as if it had a spotlight on it. The shadows and silhouettes of the 200 year old headstones presented an amazing spectacle for the eyes.

I'll never forget what happened next. It was a moment that would permanently change my life.

A green mist began to float around the headstone closest to the wall, which was maybe 50 feet away from me. The mist was like a brilliant glow. It was green, but not neon green. In fact, the self- illuminating mist had a meadow green hue to it.

The mist began to swirl like a cyclone forming, only much slower and less organized. Eventually the mist started to make a formation, and the formation began turning into a full-bodied apparition of a beautiful woman.

She was barefoot, but she didn't need shoes because her feet never touched the ground. She hovered maybe three inches in the air. I was shocked and mystified… and even a little horrified.

I grabbed my Dad's arm and shouted: "DAD!! DAD!! LOOK!!"

He turned and saw the ghostly apparition. We both stood there and stared at the phenomenon transpiring before our eyes. Was it the cold that was playing tricks on our eyes? Back then, I wasn't sure, but now I know it was real.

She was attractive and wore a long, flowing white dress and a colonial style hat that women were known to wear while doing housework back in the eighteenth century, and her long hair flowed down underneath the hat past her shoulders. She hovered around the headstone, looking first at her feet and then to the sky. On her final turn around the stone, she was looking straight ahead at us. Her eyes caught mine and we made direct eye contact which I found myself unable to break. She stopped and stared straight at me. She continued to look me right in the eye, but she never said anything.

Then she started to move forward, coming straight at us. While she moved, she raised her arm and pointed it at us. She came closer and closer to the wall. In only a moment or two, she was twenty feet away from me.

I was paralyzed from fright and I knew she was just about to go past the wall and leave the cemetery.

As she got to the wall, though, she stopped. She looked at the wall then she glanced back at me. She put one arm down to her side slowly, and then she gave us a smile.

When she reached the wall, she suddenly disappeared in a slight explosion. There was no noise, but the mist dispersed just like someone blowing out a candle on a birthday cake.

The minute she was gone, I could move again, and the surroundings became calm and quiet. The strange feeling was completely gone, and I felt a sigh of relief. Despite what I had seen and how frightening it was, the woman's smile had given me an odd calmness. It was forever burned in my brain. Even today, I can still see it if I close my eyes.

I looked at my father. He seemed paralyzed with fear.

I said: "Dad, did you just see that?"

I think my question roused him out of his state of shock, because he fumbled for his car keys in a jerky manner, quickly found the right key and started to unlock the door. All he said was: "I saw nothing. I don't know what you saw, but I saw nothing. Now, get in! We're late!"

He became very abrupt. He opened my door, waited until I got in; then he closed it behind me before walking to his side of the car. The drive to our house was very quiet; almost an awkward silence if you will.

I started to doubt what I had seen. I thought: "If Dad didn't see it, and there was no way he could miss it, then maybe I was just daydreaming."

My dad never lied to me, but this incident felt so real and horrifying it had to be real. I thought: "Could this be the first lie he's told me? Dad swears nobody should lie, regardless how bad the truth is."

Then I thought about his reaction when I asked him if he had seen what I saw. He was startled initially, and then he busied himself with finding the key to his car like he was trying to forget what happened. I thought: "Why is he acting like this if he didn't see anything?"

I knew what I had seen, I saw a ghost. It was the elusive "Green Lady" ghost!

My father, however, would never admit to what we saw that night. At first, I thought he would eventually explain it to me when I was just a little older, but every time I would bring it up, he would change the subject. I knew that someday I would prove that what I had seen was real. I didn't know how I would do it, but I would. Maybe then he would finally admit it.

During the following weeks, I told my friends at school about what I had seen. They all laughed at me, and they said I was lying. My teachers got wind of it and being a Lutheran school, they scolded me for talking such nonsense. They insisted that what I described was not what I saw. Their exact words were: "You couldn't see a ghost, because they don't exist. So stop spreading such lies!" They even threatened me with punishment if they heard me mention it again.

I complied, but that incident really bothered me. I didn't tell anyone or talk of it again.

Now, let's jump to 1993. I had been in Florida with my parents for almost three years. I still visited the cemetery with my grandfather every time I went back to Connecticut, but I would never mention what happened on that night six years before; and I could tell he wasn't about to answer any questions regarding the apparition despite hearing rumors about it for decades.

My brother and I spent that entire summer with Grandpa and Ama. It was not a nice visit because I knew my parents were in the process of getting a divorce back in Florida.

One afternoon that summer, I happened to be visiting my aunt and uncle at their home. I saw something that made me realize that I could get the evidence I needed to validate my experience. You have to keep in mind that the Internet hadn't really arrived back then, so I didn't have the resources like I do today to research the Green Lady Cemetery. All along, I had a feeling I would find the evidence in an unusual place. My evidence appeared when I spotted a book on my Aunt's coffee table. The title of the book was *Hauntings in Connecticut*.

I picked it up and browsed through it. I quickly found a section about the Green Lady Cemetery. There, in black and white, stood the proof I was looking for. The text read: "A green mist coming out of Elizabeth's stone would swirl, eventually taking on the shape of woman in a long dress and house hat. She would walk aimlessly, and if she saw you she would smile. Nobody ever saw her outside the walls of the cemetery."

I finally stopped thinking I was crazy. From that very moment, I knew I had seen a real ghost in that old cemetery, back in 1987.

The more I think about it; maybe my father didn't see the ghost. When hauntings occur, not everyone present sees a spirit, but they can be influenced by the energy it manifests. His trance-like state could have been the results from that. He may not have been lying. Once I saw the book on my aunt's coffee table, I was so pleased to finally have an answer about the legendary "Green Lady Ghost" of the "Seventh Day Baptist Cemetery".

Green Lady Cemetery
(My wife outside our car)

Elizabeth's grave is the large one to the right of my wife. The stone was stolen in 2011. This is what the cemetery looks like today

Chapter 6 – A Warning Not Heeded

It was almost the start of summer break as we entered the first week of June in 1988. Let me say that it had not been a good year thus far. My grandmother had just sustained a severe heart attack. The attack blew a quarter-size hole in the wall of her heart, and her doctors told us to be prepared for the worst. Most people don't survive heart attacks of that magnitude.

I will never forget that morning for the rest of my life. Mom told me the bad news right before I went to school. I was nine years old at the time, so I understood what she told me. I knew Ama was in trouble.

We all prepared ourselves mentally for what life would be like after the loss of the matriarch of my mother's side of the family. However, I didn't feel she was going anywhere. I had this gut feeling she would pull through the ordeal, despite the damage to her heart that she had suffered.

Sure, I prayed. I still had to come to terms with the fact that my grandmother might not make it. I thought: "I am only human, and my gut feeling could be wrong." I told everybody not to worry, but I asked about Ama every day. She was a huge figure in my life, and I loved her dearly.

One day when we were visiting her at the hospital, my mother took me to the gift shop. I used some money I had earned from my paper route to buy Ama a stuffed bear. I gave it to her to for comfort in the midst of her life and death battle. I laid my heart in that bear, and I hoped she could feel it when she had it by her side. It was my way of being there with her when she was scared, to help her realize she had so much to live for. We called the bear "Bradley" after the tag it had on its leg.

I guess my instincts were right, because Ama woke up and survived, baffling the doctors. She would later tell me she had Jesus watching over her. She also said that she wanted to live to see her three oldest grandkids graduate from high school; and if God willing, also see the rest of her grandkids graduate.

She was up and functioning, but she wasn't able to leave the hospital, and she wasn't out of the woods yet… so much could still go wrong. In all she would be in there about month so she could grow stronger and have doctors near her at a moment's notice.

My parents, my brother and I would visit her often. It was strange going to my grandparents' house every Friday without Ama being there. I would sit on my favorite chair and watch Nickelodeon while eating dinner off of a TV tray. Out of habit, I would look over to glance at Ama reading her Bible or knitting, but her chair was empty.

Three weeks went by and school was let out for the summer. I had big plans for my summer vacation. I was about to take a test for my brown belt in karate… only one level shy of being a black belt. I was also supposed to spar in a statewide karate tournament. In addition, my mom and dad were going to take us camping at Lake George, New York. I was hopeful of that summer being the best one yet.

During this time I had another recurring dream. This one involved me as well, but it was always about a severe injury that would happen to me while I was riding my bike on a sunny summer evening. Of course, I blew it off like I did most of my dreams.

As school ended, the dream of my being injured came to me three times that month. Suddenly, it came to me every night. It started on a Friday night and continued through the following Monday night… June 27, 1988.

It is still a vivid memory. I can remember it like it was yesterday.

My Bicycle Accident Dream

It is mid-morning, and I just got home from karate class. With only two weeks until the test for my brown belt and a competition, I was attending karate sessions twice a day, three days a week to prepare.

After I come home, I take off my karate gi (workout uniform) and run downstairs to play with my brand new WWF wrestler toy that I had saved all winter to buy. It was Jake “The Snake” Roberts. It had cost me more than most of the other WWF figures, because I had to buy it out of a catalog. It was an item that was unavailable in the stores.

I set up a pretend wrestling ring on my father's pool table in the basement. When I turn on the pool light above the table, it looks just like stadium floor. I turn off the rest of the lights in the basement and my make believe ring is illuminated just like a real wrestling event.

I am staging a battle between WWF stars Nikolai Volkoff and Jake “The Snake” Roberts. I can’t finish the match because it is 3:00 PM, and I have to go collect money for my paper route. I do that every Tuesday and the customers usually wait for me by their front doors.

Since I am in a rush, I leave the wrestlers in the official WWF play ring, so I can take up where I left off when I return. I run upstairs. I gather up my receipt book and my money pouch, and then I run outside to get my bike and pedal down the street.

My route isn't that large. Most of the customers who pay directly to me are far down the street… about two miles. To a nine-year-old, two miles is a long way. I love collecting the money though, because I get an opportunity to meet and talk with my customers. Many of them are elderly and love to talk.

One customer who lives in an old run-down- looking house across from the police station gives the best tips. Right behind the house is a new apartment complex and next to that are the police station and a strip mall with a bakery where my customer works. I have to collect from him at the bakery.

He usually gives a hot “right out of the oven” donut as a tip. MMMM!

This time, however, he gives me cash for a tip. This doesn't bother me at all. Either the pastry or the cash are awesome in my book, but it is odd for him to pay cash.

I finish my collecting duties around 4:00 P.M. I always collect two days a week because there are always some that I miss, so I also collect on Thursday.

After collecting I ride home with my money on my belt. It is a fun ride home because Connecticut has hills, and it is so much fun to be able to coast down them. I race up the hill as fast as I can and then as I reach the crest of the hill, I take my feet off the pedals and coast down the hill.

I pull up to my house around 4:15 to 4:20 PM. I park my bike with the front of it facing forward towards the garage, in the middle of the driveway on an oil slick. I go inside and wash up, because Mom always has dinner ready for us promptly at 5:00 P.M. On this particular day, my dad has to work late.

My mother makes ham with corn and mashed potatoes for dinner. I sit on the left side of the couch eating off a fold away table. It is summer, and the setting sun beats down on my head from the picture window facing west, warming the living room with the last beams of light for the day.

I really want to go outside and ride my bike before dark, so I inhale my food. My brother decides to ride with me, and he follows me outside after he is done eating. Before I go outside, though, I remember that that I didn't finish my wrestling match from earlier, but the gorgeous summer evening beckons me.

My brother and I go outside; and there is my bike just as I left it, parked on the oil slick. My brother has to get his from the garage. While he is getting his bike out and jumping on it, I have already made my way down the driveway onto Homestead Lane. It is a dead end street, so I never have to worry about cars.

After a few passes up and down the street, my brother and I decide to go onto Old Turnpike Road, something we are forbidden to do unless I was on my paper route. That is the

ONLY time I have permission to go on that busy street and even at that, I have to stay on the sidewalk.

The sidewalk stands about four inches above the road, so if a car hits the sidewalk, it will bounce off before coming onto the walk. This will give pedestrians and bicyclists time to react. However, boys will be boys, and we decide to stay on the smooth tar of the busy road.

We go past my neighbor's house and we are about to turn onto the sidewalk and follow that back to our street, when a blue Buick comes barreling down the road. I am closest to the sidewalk and my brother is on my left nearest the street.

No two kids can peddle their bikes any faster than we do to avoid the car, but the older lady who is driving does not swerve to avoid us. In order to avoid being hit, my brother merges his bike towards me, which pushes his peddle into my chain.

That locks my chain. The front wheel of my bike turns 45 degrees to the right. I am thrown head first over my handle bars. I put my arms out to protect my head and soften the blow of the rough landing I am about to experience.

As I move forward to brace the fall, one of my hands turns at a 45 degree angle, twisting my arm. The momentum of my body continuing towards the ground locks my hand solid against the ground, forcing my elbow to hyperextend and bend inward like a fragile bird's leg would do.

The impact snaps my arm like a twig. The fracture allows my shoulder to touch my hand and the backside of my forearm to touch the backside of my upper arm. At first I lay there in shock and disbelief but it becomes all too real after I stand up and my arm dangles around.

I sustain a compound fracture that shatters the joint. The bone fragments char my muscle tissue and I have no feeling in my arm, and no ability to lift it at all. Luckily, it is my left arm, since I am right handed.

I manage to get up. I hold my arm with my right hand. I scream out of sheer terror. I don't know what to think. Losing all feeling in an arm or the ability to move it is horrific for anybody, but it is magnified for a nine year old.

My mother rushes me to Southington Hospital. Then, she calls my dad and tells him to get home right away.

And then… I wake up.

Reality is an Imitation of a Dream

June 28th, 1988 was a Tuesday which started out just the way it did in the dream I had been having every night. When I got home from karate class, I went downstairs to play with my wrestlers. I had the same two figures in the ring. At 3:00 P.M., my mom yelled down to me: "STOP WHAT YOU'RE DOING AND GO COLLECT THE MONEY FROM YOUR ROUTE!" At that moment, I had a flashback of my recurrent dream, but I ignored it.

When the man who gave me a donut gave me cash as opposed to the usual yummy donut as a tip, I had another flashback. Again I ignored it.

When I sat down to eat dinner, I noticed that the food on my plate as the same as in my dream, I had my third flashback. Once again, I ignored it.

When I went outside to get my bike to ride, it was parked in the same spot and the same oil slick as in my dream. At this point, I saw and felt the strongest *de ja vu* flashback of that day, but I ignored it because I wanted to go play. I wish I had paid attention because it was a warning not taken.

By 5:30P.M., I had broken my arm in the exact same fashion my dream predicted I would.

I was rushed to the hospital. I was told I would need surgery. The compound fracture had resulted in, for all intents and purposes, an amputation. The only thing holding my left arm together was my skin. As you can imagine, I did not sleep well that night.

My parents asked me if I wanted to go to Bristol Hospital, the same one I was born in and the one where my grandmother still was at. I said: “No, I’m fine here. I trust them. They’ll do a good job.”

At 9:00 AM the next morning, my heart sank as the orderlies came to take me off to surgery. There is nothing more intimidating than looking up at people in white carrying you down to cut you open. It’s a vision you won’t soon forget.

After that moment, I don't remember much except the surgeon allowed me to knock myself out with a strawberry flavored anesthesia mask. That was cool.

Afterwards, my parents filled me in on what had happened. They told me the surgery had taken eight hours. The doctors were able to put my arm together with pins that would eventually come out with another surgery. I lost the muscle in the back of my arm because of the bone fragments, I would have limited movement, and I had lost a lot of arm strength. The doctors also figured that by the time I was 30, I would start to get arthritis in the joint since the cartilage was destroyed.

I was heavily medicated for a couple of days, and I was very weak. My karate instructor came to visit me and he brought me some foam Chinese throwing stars I had been eye balling at his school, as well as a set of foam practice nunchucks. I was awake briefly for his stay. But a day later I got the best visit ever!

My parents managed to get me up, and sitting at the foot of my bed was my grandmother! She was so weak and frail but she smiled and that smile lit the room up for me. She just rubbed my foot and leg while my grandfather sat on a chair by my bed.

I cried out: “AMA!” Was I glad to see her.!

She nodded, and said: “You had to go and bang yourself up, huh? I wasn't expecting us to both be held up this summer.”

I smiled and fell back asleep. It was such a relief to know she was OK! I truly believe her visit made me recover faster.

Time seemed to drag by until I was finally released from the hospital. My summer had really been blown off because the accident happened just three days into my summer break. I had a cast on from the tips of my fingers to my shoulder. My camping trip was in jeopardy of not happening. As far as the karate tournament was concerned, forget about it. I could still take the test for my brown belt, but the test was still contingent on me performing without a sling.

I visited with my grandmother often that summer. We played cards, I taught her a new card game I learned in school and we watched a LOT of television. Because of the medications she was on, she was always hot. So, she placed a window AC unit in the living room, and we chilled out... literally.

As for me, I was told if I could not lift my arm without a sling I could not participate in the tournament. That hope was gone, but I did manage to pass my brown belt test. At that time, I watched a black belt with my name be placed on the wall, which was the tradition when a student achieved the level of brown belt because it gave them a visual reminder and something to shoot for.

I had to spar in order to be awarded a brown belt. I managed to compete by putting my left arm, which was in the cast, behind my back to protect it and fought one handed. I scored two points of three, but finally lost the battle. I think I gained a lot of respect from my classmates and the instructors that night. I was mad, though, because, prior to my accident, I had only lost three matches out of 80 in my life, and this one was the fourth. Still in all, I passed the test and received my brown belt in karate. Life was starting to get a little better.

A few weeks later, my cast was reduced to a normal size cast, and it was also waterproofed so I could go camping. During the camping trip, I was chased by some animal and tripped and fell over a branch while trying to get away. The rough landing forced the pins to come through my elbow skin.

By August, the cast was completely off, and I only needed an ace bandage to cover the exposed pins. When I went back to school the first week of September, the kids liked to see the exposed pins, and I had no problem showing them. They also liked the huge scar I had down my elbow.

I had the pins removed a week into school. After six months of physical therapy, I managed to regain 90% range of motion in my arm. I never would regain the full range of motion. I still have the scar today to remind me of that horrific summer evening.

The doctors were right about the arthritis. I had no side effects really until I hit 30. The only discomfort I experience is that my arm aches when it rains but I've noticed that arthritis is starting to form in the joint. I am really very lucky.

Ama passed away in 1999. She got her wish. She saw all three of her eldest grandkids graduate. She died the day the state of Connecticut gave my cousin her graduation letter. My cousin received her diploma a few hours after we buried Ama.

When everyone went through her belongings, I took two things. A bear I had bought for her at a Catskill Game Farm in New York's Catskill's and the bear I gave her in the hospital, which had since been since renamed "Lucky".

Ama had renamed it Lucky when she went into congestive heart failure in the mid 90s, and she threw the bear at my grandfather… it was the only thing that woke him up. If she had not awakened him, we would have lost her a lot sooner.

That summer of 1988 made me realize one major thing: Trust your instincts, trust your dreams and if you experience a *de ja vu* moment, or warning of some kind... heed its warning! I learned a hard lesson, and I never again took those warnings for granted.

Here is a fun fact: The movie *A Haunting in Connecticut* took place in Southington, Connecticut. In fact, I passed right by that house every day while delivering papers. My momentous summer of 1988 was also the time when everything culminated for the family of that house. Her son and I were at the same hospital that summer, me for my arm and him for his chemo.

"Lucky"

Chapter 7 – My Dad's Business Career: Lofty Peaks and Deep Valleys

My dad was once a very successful man. At one time he was making so much money that he had hopes of retiring at the age of 34.

After he received his Associate's degree from a community college in Winsted, Connecticut, my dad worked as an engineering assistant for Pratt and Whitney. His mother had a friend who was a nurse down at the Pratt and Whitney aircraft plant in West Palm Beach, Florida. He took a job as an engineering assistant and moved to Florida. That was how he originally got down to the Sunshine State.

By this time, he had met my mom and fallen in love. He was able to get a transfer back to Connecticut. He worked in the Pratt and Whitney's fuel cell division at a facility outside of Hartford. It wasn't too long after that when he decided to get into the investment business. He had always had an interest in investments. He had played penny stocks and had done quite well at it.

Right after my mom and dad got married, my dad bought a house in Burlington, Connecticut, a suburb west of Hartford. They moved out there because it was so peaceful and quiet. This was in 1976. They paid $70,000 for it, which was a sizeable sum back then.

It was a raised ranch style home located on George Washington Turnpike, which sounds like a busy road, but was really a dead end street out in the woods. The house was about 250 feet off the road. It had two ponds. If you went out the back door and looked into the backyard, you would see 350 acres of the Nassahegon State Forest.

The outside of the house needed staining, so my dad undertook that project. When he began working around the front door, he noticed all this putty. He wondered what that was about. It was hot, and he decided to get a beer. He told my mom he'd be gone five minutes and went into town.

Back then, Burlington was very small and in fact, it still is. It might have had 900 people at the time. It had a general store, a volunteer fire department, a church, a mom and pop hardware store and a liquor store… that was it. He got into a conversation with the proprietor of the liquor store and mentioned the house he had just purchased. The owner of the liquor store said: "Oh, you bought the 'rifleman's' house!" The proprietor proceeded to fill my dad in on a history of the house, and my dad didn't get home for two hours.

The Saga of the Rifleman's House

The man who built the house my dad had bought was a Vietnam War vet and a highly-trained sniper. He had married a Vietnamese woman and brought her back to the states. One day, he discovered that she had been cheating on him. He went crazy.

There were two houses which were closer to the road than his. He used his rifle to blow the telephone right off the wall in the house to the left of our home. He threatened to kill his wife and children, and he shot the neighbor's phone out in order to prevent them from calling the authorities. They had a jalousie back porch, and a wall phone was mounted on that porch. It was a clean shot made from his house. He didn't injure anybody. He just didn't want anybody making any more calls.

Anyway, he held off the state police for six hours. They riddled the house with bullets. It was amazing that they did that because the Vietnam vet had the kids in a back room. The only way they finally got him out of the house was by driving an Army National Guard tank up the driveway. They blew off part of the roof, which explained why part of the roof was redone before my dad bought the place.

Anyhow, the state police took the vet alive. Nobody was hurt. It had to have made the news, but my dad had never heard anything about it.

The owner of the liquor store also told my dad that the house was supposedly booby trapped and wired with explosives. My dad didn't see any wires after he returned home. He did notice that downstairs in the basement or family room, the Vietnam vet had built a walk in closet. All of the shelves were made from boxes used to ship projectiles in. The vet had also left behind a lamp that had been made for a bullet used in a tank. He also left a photo of his purple heart with a bullet hole in the center of it.

The basement was laid out in an odd manner. The Vietnam vet had built the basement room with a fireplace in the corner, which didn't allow people to sit around it. One day, my dad was playing tennis with his brother-in-law and said: "One day, I'm going to take out a wall in the basement and open it up for a fireplace." His brother-in-law went ahead and knocked the wall down while my dad was away on a trip.

After my dad returned, he was throwing stuff from the basement out the back and he found wiring. It turned out the house *was* wired after all. Fortunately, the wiring wasn't connected to any explosives. Evidently, the Vietnam vet was paranoid and suicidal. He was planning to go out in a blaze of glory.

My dad never knew any of this and his realtor never told him any of this. He never bothered the realtor about it once he found out because it was really a case of "no harm, no foul". The proprietor of the liquor store was related to the person who developed the property that those three houses were on. All in all, it was a strange situation that became a hidden secret.

My Dad's Great Success as a Financial Planner

My dad ended up going to work for Paine Webber. He had to do some traveling, so my parents decided to move closer to the city. That's when they sold the house in Burlington and moved to

Southington. My dad was still into ski boats and all kinds of stuff back then.

He began to specialize in all aspects of financial planning. My dad started a company called Financial Design. He did so well that he started a spinoff company called Security Financial, which was a big financial planning firm. He also had Financial Attitudes, which was a stock brokerage firm and had Security Assurance Services, which was a life and health insurance agency. In 1979, he was written up in *Money* magazine as one of the Top 200 Financial Counselor in the Country.

He was on a roll and decided to take his company public and sell the stock. He had a deal in the works for Bank of Boston to buy his shares. He was truly at a point where he would have been able to retire at age 34.

Just when he went to close out the deal, my dad discovered that his attorney had embezzled all the escrow money. He not only robbed my dad, he also stole a bunch of money belonging to other people. My dad ended up going bankrupt trying to pay everybody back. He had a fiduciary responsibility to do that. The mess also triggered an investigation by the Securities and Exchange Commission, departments of banking in five states and the International Association of Security Dealers. It cost Dad $185,000 to be proven innocent. He went from $30,000 a month to nothing in ninety days. Needless to say, my father went through some terrible times.

My dad went to work selling life and health insurance and was transferred to Florida. He was based out of Tampa. He covered a region consisting of Florida, Alabama and Mississippi. He picked Land O'Lakes to live in because it was centrally located to Tampa International Airport and, at the time, Land O'Lakes was known for its public schools. Nowadays, Land O'Lakes is best known for being the Nudist Resort Capitol of America, with three such resorts.

We moved out of Connecticut just a week before Christmas, I will never forget because it was going to be the first Christmas without all of my extended family around us.

I quickly realized that Florida wasn't like the brochures I had seen. In fact, it almost looked like the complete opposite of what was depicted. I was expecting miles of beautiful beaches, beautifully manicured lawns grass and gorgeous homes. Sure, Florida has all those things, but not where we relocated to.

Coming to the Tampa Bay area was a cultural shock for me, to say the least. I've been here ever since, but I never lost my northern blood. Florida is not a place where I can live easily, because I still can’t get used to the heat and humidity.

Coming here resulted in a complete change in my life, but at the time, I never realized how much of an impact it would have. I didn’t begin realize how much my life would change until the summer of 1992.

Chapter 8 – A Demon Inside

I still don't know what happened to cause the paranormal terrorism I was to endure, or why I was personally targeted. Maybe it was the horrific case of chicken pox I had in 7th grade. Maybe it was the fact that I was on my last year in middle school and big changes were about to transpire. Maybe it was because I was going to be confirmed in April of 1993, and that was just around the corner. Maybe it was because my parents were contemplating a divorce, which caused an influx in anger and disappointment into the household. I could go on with a list of "maybe's" all day long, but I still can't explain why. I may never know why and honestly, that's okay with me.

This incident would heighten my awareness to the paranormal. It would make me face my greatest fears and test my strength as an individual. How was this done, you ask? It happened when a fourteen-year-old child was pitted against one of the most feared paranormal entities in the known universe; one of Satan's helpers, a demon. I'll never forget the first night it made itself known.....

I was in the eighth grade at the time. It was early October and school had been in session for just about two months or so. I was in my bedroom doing my homework around 8:00 PM, as I usually did.

It is important for you to know that my bedroom was not large. My bed lay against an exterior wall with the headboard touching a sliding glass door to the porch. My desk was right next to my bed, and I had the venetian blinds closed. Next to the desk was my bedroom door, which was completely opened. If I looked over to my right while sitting at my desk, I could see right into my brother's bedroom.

His bedroom light was off because he was in my parents' bedroom playing Nintendo, and my mom was either in her bedroom with him or watching TV. My dad wasn't home yet from work. He would get home late, usually around 9:00 P.M. to 9:30 PM every night.

In other words, I was completely alone at the other end of the house. The bathroom light was off and there was really no noise at all that would have taken my attention from my studies.

Around 8:30 PM, I was really focused on my homework assignment and the desk lamp was the only thing lighting my room. I noticed my brother's light came on in his room, and I heard the sliding door to his closet open. I didn't see anyone go in his room, but it was dark and the lamp on my desk was on the corner of the desk closest to the door, so the foreground was far brighter than what could be seen in my brother's room. Due to the lighting, it would have been easy to miss someone walking in there.

I was getting anxious and I decided to take a break. The distraction was enough to convince me to get a drink from the kitchen. I never stopped looking at his bedroom, though, and I didn't see anything moving at all. Something just wasn't right, however, and I was about to find out when I got up to get my drink.

I started by looking into his room, and the perspective of his room grew wider as I crept closer to his door. As I reached the door jam, I could see his bed and it was still made, so he wasn't in the bed. I looked around the corner to check the door to his closet, and I saw that it was open, but nobody was there.

For some reason, that kind of startled me. I could feel the hairs on my neck start to stand up on end. I knew that since the moment the light went on, I had never once taken my eyes off my brother's room. I certainly would have seen someone leave.

So, I decided to go to the kitchen, get my drink and peek in on my mom and brother. She wasn't in the living room, so I went to her bedroom and found her sleeping in her bed. My brother was also on the bed, and he was sleeping as well. He had fallen asleep playing his video games.

My mom woke up and said: "Oh, I must have dozed off... is everything OK?"

She must have sensed that I was looking at her. "Yes," I replied. "I just wanted to see what was going on." I didn't dare tell her what had just happened.

I was holding my drink in my hand when I told her: "I'm going to finish my homework and then I'm going to bed." As I left the room, she replied: "Goodnight... Love you."

Let me say that was one of the longest walks back across the house I ever had. I was really hesitant to get back to my room and as I got closer to my bedroom, that eerie feeling grew even more intense. By the time I reached the small hallway that connected the two bedrooms, the hairs on my neck and arms were standing straight up.

I didn't want to look at my brother's bedroom, but I was compelled to... probably out of sheer amazement and confusion of what had happened. As I turned and looked in his room, the lights were still on, but now the sliding closet doors were closed.

When I left the room prior to going to the kitchen, I hadn't touched a thing. There was no reason for those doors to have been closed. I knew the doors could not have closed by themselves. I turned out the light and ran into my room, closing the door behind me.

My dad came home at 9:30 PM. He slept in my brother's room that night, which comforted me a bit. What I didn't know was that this was only the first of many encounters with an entity that

I would soon find out to be a demon. What I experienced that night was one of the mild haunts. Life threatening ones were soon to come.

The Floating Headphones

It was now December, and I was hoping to receive a portable CD player for Christmas. They had just come out on the market, and I had never had a CD player before. It was small enough to sit on my desk so I could listen to music while doing homework, or I could place it next to my bed while I relaxed for the night. I asked for three CDs, "*The Beach Boys: Made in the USA*", "*The Turtles' Greatest Hits*" and anything by Neil Diamond. I loved the oldies!

When I opened my presents that Christmas, I got a CD player, but I didn't get the Neil Diamond CD I wanted. I solved that problem by taking the cash I got for Christmas and purchasing a Lovin' Spoonful's CD and a Neil Diamond CD. That brought my collection up to four CDs, and I loved every one of them.

The night of December 28th, 1992 was during the period when Mom and Dad's divorce was heating up. I was getting ready for the New Year that was just around the corner and enjoying the winter break. I had homework on my winter breaks, so one night while I was working on my vacation assignment, I ran into something I needed clarification on. My dad was in my brother's room so I went there to ask him for some help.

I needed his assistance in my room, so I begged him to come in. He followed me back to my bedroom and unbeknownst to us, we were about to see a sight that would blow our minds.

When we got to the door of my bedroom, my father and I both halted. We were totally shocked at what we saw. The headphones of my CD player were floating. I could hear a faint sound coming from them, but couldn't recognize the song.

I slowly walked up to the headphones. I had a suspicion of how the headphones were able to float, but the idea was so disturbing that I didn’t want to think about it.

As I got to the headphones, I reached for them to see if I could feel anything that would be causing these headphones to float in mid air. Just as I reached for them, they suddenly dropped, slamming on the seat of my wooden chair. The music still played, though, and I found that to be a bit weird.

I listened to the headphones and heard:

“Shilo, when I was young

I used to call your name.

When no one else would come

Shilo, you always came

And we’d play.”

I recognized the cut. It was Neil Diamond's *Shilo*, a song about an imaginary friend. I hit the stop button on the CD player, but it wouldn't turn off and the music kept playing. I started to hit the stop button with more force, but the CD player still wouldn’t turn off. Finally, on one last try, it shut off. The music stopped, and I could retrieve the CD.

When I opened the lid I got the shock of my life. I must have turned pale white because my dad asked: “What's wrong? You look like you just saw a ghost”. I turned around, picked up the CD player and showed my dad the player with the lid open... there was no CD in the machine. How could a CD player produce music without a CD??

My father was a bit shocked, to say the least. He asked me: “What was the song that was played?”

I told him it was Shilo by Neil Diamond.

He said: "Okay, I give up. How did you do that trick?'

I said: "I didn't do anything, Dad. The music was playing without a CD in the player."

He was tired and was in no mood for games. He became exasperated and shouted: "STOP PLAYING WITH ME! Where did you put the CD?"

I went to my desk and pulled out the Neil Diamond CD jewel case from the CD rack, opened it and showed him the inside of the case.

"Here it is Dad, in the case where I left it".

He believed me, but my dad tries to be very scientific and practical when it comes to the paranormal. He wouldn't come right out and say that it was a ghost unless there were absolutely no other logical explanations. However in this case, he had heard the song, and the CD was in the case the whole time. What could anyone possibly say to disprove that?

The thing that really got to me about the entire incident was that my dad chalked up the phenomenon that had just taken place to something strange. He continued to believe that I had played some sort of trick on him. I wish I could say I had been playing a trick on him, but I wasn't. At that point, I realized I was in for some serious problems because there was definitely an entity in my room.

The Shadow on the Wall

After the entity showed me it was in my room by invading my space with the headphone act, it made its presence known to me every single night. Up until this point, it did this only through such comparatively minor things such as opening and closing closet doors. There were also times when some things would come up missing and then reappear in the same place I had left them. After a while, this was no longer enough for the entity. It upped the ante by revealing itself to me, while still maintaining a degree of anonymity.

From that point forward to the summer of 1993, the entity appeared to me every night in the form of a shadow of a human figure. It would enter from my closet and sit on the far left corner of my wall. I felt very negative energy in the room whenever it was about to show its face. To this day, I truly believe it was living in my closet; that somehow the closet was a portal to the other world.

The shadow would sit and stare at me every single night. I tried to ignore it, but sometimes it was impossible to do that. How could you avoid looking at something that had no physical form, but possessed large glowing eyes? It had a human form, so it was not a "beast" like you would typically associate with the idea of a demon.

I knew it was looking at me. I knew it was trying to not only communicate with me, but to scare me into doing what it asked. Had I given in to it, I would have forever been possessed by the evil being because I was of the age and mindset to understand free will. If I freely chose to do what it suggested, I would have willingly allowed it to gain control of me and make me its slave. It would have been like signing an iron-clad contact. This evil entity would have then been able to use me as a host to do its dirty work. Perhaps fear played a big part in my decision to not let this entity get the best of me, but whatever it was, I am glad I had a strong enough will to resist it, even at the age of fourteen.

I never looked directly at it, but once in a while I would glance at it. I always knew the instant it was gone because the energy in the room would lighten. I tried to sleep looking at the wall with my back to the entity; which was really my only defense.

The Demon's Physical Touch

For almost six months, the entity appeared and haunted my room, but after that sixth month, things began to change and it took its attack to a higher level. The entity actually started to get physical with me. This wasn't an everyday occurrence. It stayed pretty much the way it was… silent and haunting from afar… but every now and then it decided to show me it meant business. It made sure I knew it could hurt me, or maybe even kill me, anytime it wanted to.

I think it did this to instill fear into me so that it could take control me, or hope that I would give into its demands and thereby conquer my free will by manipulation. If you are scared of someone or something, you tend to do whatever it asks or tells you to do, just to avoid confrontation and adverse consequences.

Despite the violence, I never gave in. I stayed strong because I knew that if I let my guard down and let the entity see how scared I was, it would control me. I had no option but to endure its wrath.

From time to time the entity would first make sure I was awake before it would cause physical harm to me. If I was sleeping when it decided to attack, it made sure I woke up first. That was so I could see the power it possessed and be scared beyond scared when I looked into the holes that once held its eyes.

The demon would usually grab me with its large hands, push my head against the mattress and start to strangle me. I was pinned down and could not move it was almost like I was in a catatonic state. I saw what was going on, but my body was completely lifeless, unable to fight the attack off. Sometimes the entity would allow me to flail my arms and legs but not let me scream

I could not breathe with its hands around my throat. My lungs would start to ache, my heart would begin to beat fast and I could feel an artery in my head pound. Just when I thought I was about to pass out, the beast would pull its hands off my neck and I could feel the blood rush back through my body. My lungs would fill once again with air so quickly that it would make me cough. It would do this two more times on each occasion, toying with me like a cat would do to its prey. But unlike a predatory cat, when I was too weak to function it would leave and not kill me.

Sometimes the entity would scratch me viciously. I've been known to have Freddy Kruger-like scratches down my back… five claw marks. There were also times when I awakened with letters carved into my chest, and the letters would spell "murder". Oddly enough, it would only carve one letter at a time into me.

The back scratches and the scratches down my chest hurt like hell. I would wake up to find the letters carved into me, and I could never remember it happening. Either way, both sets of scratches would disappear within 24 hours.

The hand prints from the choking and the scratch marks made it very difficult for me to go to school and dress out for P.E. I found a way to trick the teachers to make it seem like I dressed out, so I wouldn't fail. Dressing out in P.E. class was fifty percent of my grade.

I would wear two sets of clothes to school on the days I had P.E. classes. I wore street clothes much larger than my regular size over a sweat shirt or t-shirt and a pair of running shorts. I would go into a bathroom stall and take my outer layer of clothes before P.E. class. Since the coaches saw me come to class with street clothes on and then saw me in class wearing a sweatshirt or t-shirt and shorts, they had no idea what I was up to. It was difficult at times, but I managed.

I went to all that trouble because I could only imagine what would have happened if someone in authority had seen the scratches and hand marks around my neck and back. They would swear my parents were beating and mutilating me and should be prosecuted for child abuse. But in truth, Mom and Dad were not abusing me. How would I explain to a teacher, principal or social worker that my wounds were caused by a ghost? That story definitely wouldn't fly.

One night, the ghost grabbed me by my neck, pulled me out of bed and pinned me against the wall. I was about six to seven inches above my bed, pressed against the wall and trying to swallow despite the demon's strong, thick hands. I couldn't believe the power it possessed.

The entire situation put me under enormous stress. I didn't want to bring any of my friends over because I didn't want this thing to hurt them. It rarely showed itself during the day, but still... what if it did.

One Friday night, I took the risk and invited a friend over to spend the night, even though the demon might show itself. He slept on a cot set up next to my bed. We stayed up and told funny stories, talked about girls and had other typical boy conversations.

My worst fear happened at midnight when the demon showed itself. It stayed pressed against the wall, staring out at us with those oval slanted eyes, but there were no eye balls in the sockets. We couldn't make out what it was. We knew it had human qualities, but all we could see was just a shadow.

My friend asked me how I was making that shadow and I said to him in a hesitant manner: "It isn't me."

He laughed and threw his shoe at it. That was probably the worst mistake he ever made.

That demon disappeared from the wall, and it began making a loud deep growling noise. My friend looked around the room, and then turned a pale white. At that very instant, the demon reappeared, grabbed him by his neck and slammed him against the wall.

I was helpless. I could see my friend grasping the demon's hand, trying to free himself from the grip of the demonic entity. Finally, the demon let loose of him, and then threw him against the floor. Miraculously, my friend wasn't hurt. He got up off the floor and ran right to the bathroom.

He asked me: "What was that?"

I broke down. I let him in on the secret I had been keeping and told him everything. I told him what the evil demon had done to me physically, and I asked if he wanted to stay in another room. He said no, but he never returned for a sleep over again.

What blew my mind most about that incident was that, at the time, my friend and I were eighth graders; and he was just about 6 foot 1 inches tall and was about 220 pounds. I was 5 foot 6 inches tall and 125 pounds soaking wet. It horrified me to see how much strength that demon had, and to witness what it did to my friend. Because of that, I stopped inviting friends over to my house.

Ghost in my Bed

There was a rare instance when the demon did not target me. In fact, I had no idea this was even going on at the time.

My brother had gone to his bedroom, and I guess he had a question or something for me, so he decided to come get me. He thought I was in my bedroom. In fact, I was watching Nick at Night's *Get Smart* in the living room.

When he got into my bedroom, he saw what he thought was me sleeping in my bed, on my side. The pillow was caved in like a head was on it, and the outline of the body looked like someone was sleeping on their side.

My brother came over to the bed and went to shake me awake, as he put his hand on what he thought was my arm. Upon touching the sheet, the sheets collapsed as if there were nothing under them, scaring my brother half to death. He ran out of my room screaming. By the time he got to the living room, he was coherent enough to tell me what had happened.

I explained what was going on in my room, and warned him it was best to stay away from my room at night. I began trying to stay up as long as I could by watching TV all night, every night. Obviously, this didn't help my performance in school.

An Out of Body Experience

It was almost the start of summer break, 1993. I was about to start high school the next year, and my parents were just about to send us up north as they went to get their divorce.

Things were really bad in the house. My dad was going through huge problems on his job. Right after that, he got fired. Then, everything came to a head. That's when my mom said: "Enough is enough," and my parents divorced.

Tensions were high, there was lots of arguing and the negative energy was so thick you could cut it with a knife. It was the perfect breeding grounds for the evil entity that was tormenting me.

The more I think about it, I firmly believe that the evil entity had a lot to do with my family's destruction. I think it caused my dad to do the things he did, which ultimately broke up the family. It even affected my brother. I believe the demon did all this because that is what diabolical entities do.

Anyway, I had gone to bed late. I had been staying up late because I was excited about graduating from middle school, and I was anticipating high school. It was a Friday night, so staying up late wasn't really a problem. When I went to bed that night, I had no idea what I was in for.

It was around 1:00 AM. The demon did the most amazing thing yet. It pulled my spirit from my body while I was sleeping. I found myself hovering in the air above my bed. I could only stare in disbelief as I looked at my own body sleeping. I didn't know if I was dead, but I did see my chest breathing.

I looked behind me only to see the demon in its true state … it wasn't just a shadow anymore. It looked like a well groomed human, with ripping muscles and giant hands and extremities. It was very handsome, but it had horns growing out of its head. It wasn't scary for me at all to see this demon, in fact this being possessed such charisma that I could easily how it could manipulate a person and gain their trust.

The demon grabbed me by the back of my neck and called me by my name. It said: “Jason, we're going to go see your mother.” Then, it pulled me by my neck with such force that it was caving my neck in.

It took me to my mother's room where my brother and mother were sleeping. It forced my head down close to my mother and said in a sneering, beastly tone: “See her? I am going to kill her.” Then it took me over to my brother and said the same thing. Then, it took me to my brother's room where my dad was sleeping and made the same threat about my father.

I actually started to tear up, because I didn't want anything to happen to them. The demon then showed me what it was going to look like after he killed my family, and what a void I was going to live in.

Then it said: “Because you are not listening to me, your family must pay the price for your stubbornness and unwillingness to cooperate.” The demon went on to tell me how enraged it was with me and how stupid I had been for playing games with it. It told me that after it was done killing my family and toying with me, then it was going to destroy me.

That only made me angry. In fact, it was the first time I really cared about what this entity was doing. I didn't care what it did to me, but I was determined that it would not hurt my family. I thought it was bluffing; that it was using the threat of harming my family as a way to convince me to do what it wanted me to do; but I wasn't about to find out and I sure as hell wasn't going to give in either.

According to the Bible, God says that demons cannot kill you. They can cause things that will hurt and harm you, but they can't take your life. However, if your body can't take the abuse you sustain from their attacks, then I suppose that they could contribute to your death. But a demon can't kill you directly. That's probably why it let go of me after it had been choking me.

When it was finished with me for the night, the demon placed my spirit back into my body, and I awoke gasping for air. I ran into my dad's bedroom and screamed for him, but, as loud as I was yelling, he wouldn't wake up. I did the same for my mother, but like my dad, she too didn't wake up. I thought I was dead.

I went into the living room to calm down and figure out what I needed to do. I turned on the TV and watched *Nick at Night*. I was there for fifteen minutes when my mother came into the room, turned off the TV and left; never looking at me at all. It was almost as if she thought someone had left the set on. She acted as though I wasn't even there.

At that point, I started to panic. I screamed "MOM!!" and she turned around and looked at me. Thankfully, she had finally heard me. She scolded me, and told me to get to bed. Normally I would have been upset, but to see her react to me made me happy because I knew I wasn't dead.

Over the next few weeks, I read the Bible every night. I learned that through Christ's death, He became the ultimate sacrifice. Through His blood, He conquered death and defeated the Devil in Hell. That being said, upon His departure and through His death, we are now able to command these entities to leave. Commanding a demon to leave is not an easy task at all, but demons can be controlled. And I was preparing to do just that.

The Exorcism: My Deliverance

It took a few weeks to gain the strength to challenge the beast. I was scared because if I failed, I could only imagine what the consequences would be. My family was at stake, and I could not let them down. I was tired and fed up with the antics the demon was putting me through.

One dark Saturday night, the beast appeared in my room, just like it did every night. This time, however, as opposed to rolling over in my bed and sleeping, I got up, grabbed my Bible and held it to my heart.

I commanded the entity in the name of Jesus Christ to leave my room and my residence. I recited Psalms from the Bible in between my rebuking the evil creature.

The entity grew very aggravated. The energy in the room would have smothered a bear. The entity started to grab my neck and choke me, but I did not stop reading the word of God, despite how hard it was becoming to breathe and speak.

It then punched and slapped me, scratched me and threw me around the room; but I kept coming back. I was determined that the beast would be gone that night!

I struggled with it for almost 45 minutes. I demanded that it reveal its name and continued reading the crucifixion of Christ. I heard it say: "Your God can not help you now," as it laughed.

I replied: "In the name of Jesus Christ, I command you to leave this house, this room and return to Hell."

It said: "I know who Jesus is. He cannot help you right now."

The beast was growing weaker, though. I could sense that, as it made desperate efforts to make me stop the process.

Finally, I trapped the beast's shadow in between my two closets with sliding doors. There was a divider wall about 24 inches wide between the two storage spaces. The shadow lay flat against the divider wall, taunting me and saying: "Is this all you've got?"

As it stood there, I grabbed my Bible and ran up to the wall. I took the Bible, and placed it on the shadow, saying: "In the name of Jesus Christ, and the power he gave to me over you upon His death and resurrection, I command you back to Hell!"

That was all I needed to do. Once the Bible touched the entity, God took over. He sent His angels down to take the entity from my home and cast it into the pits of Hell. As I placed the Bible up against the shadow, I was amazed to see it sucked through the Bible and down my arm through the floor.

Needless to say, the entire experience was surreal. The beast felt cold as it passed through me. And as it passed through me, another amazing thing happened. I saw a female apparition, and I felt a female presence. There was sorrow all around her. I could read her thoughts. I saw life through her eyes… it was a life of profound sorrow. I could almost live her life for her, and I truly wanted to. That's how intense it was. The scratches and bruises disappeared too.

I thought I had messed up the exorcism because, with those feelings, I thought the monstrous demon had taken possession of me. The incident made me almost completely turn into a hermit. I didn't want anyone to know what had happened. How could I tell ANYONE that I MIGHT BE POSSESSED?? Could you imagine the criticism I would take? Life would not be worth living.

That made for a rough high school career, but somehow I made it through. I set my sights on graduation and doing the best I could in school.

From that day forward I never saw the being again. In September, after school started, my mom, brother and I moved into a town home down the street.

That incident also intensified my ability to feel and read energy from people. I could now look at someone and tell if they were a good person or a bad person. When I first realized what I could do, it really freaked me out. I could also touch people and see their entire life, their emotions and much more. Ironically I could do it all along, and that explained why I had seen ghosts. At that point, my eyes were opened to my full potential. It was a gift from God, but I would not realize it till I was much older.

This had a negative effect on me. I stopped touching people, even with a handshake, unless I absolutely had to. I found that crowds breed different energies, so being around crowds made it very difficult for me because I could hear and see the pasts, presents and futures of so many individuals making up the crowd, plus the noise was very hard to shut off.

I had always known I had psychic-like abilities, but now it was ten times stronger than ever before. I could see auras, past memories, emotions… you name it. It was a trip, to say the least… a wild, wild ride.

My psychic ability had also put me at odds with my religion and their beliefs all during the time I was growing; but I never once lost faith in God and Jesus. The Bible has prophets, but they were chosen by God to see the future for a specific reason.

The Bible says demons exist, so the fact that I had dealt with the evil entity didn't challenge my religion. On the other hand, having the ability to see life through the eyes of a woman who was a full-bodied apparition put me at odds with Lutheranism. I had been taught not to believe in reincarnation and not to believe that after death, a soul can stay behind in this world and communicate with the living.

This caused a lot of heartache and confusion for me. I asked myself: "Is everything I learned through school wrong?

But then I thought: "We are only human. Nobody knows what happens when we die, so maybe there is truth to what I am experiencing."

My Theory of What Happened

This incident brought me to a conclusion that, in life, there is a perfect balance of good and evil. Everything involves something good and something not so good… winning and losing, profits and losses, highs and lows, etc These two opposing elements must exist for life to continue. Tipping the scales to one side or the other can lead to catastrophic ramifications.

I believe these two worlds… the world of good and the world of evil… meet at a common line. That line is the earth. Being here on earth, I believe that at certain times we can transcend the portal of life and death and experience the dead among us.

I also believe that God will cast his children into Hell if they chose to not obey what He asks and do not believe that Jesus Christ died for our sins. I now know that, without question, Hell exists.

It is my belief that the earth was given to Satan to control, and he will control the earth until Jesus comes again. To this day, I do not believe we can see human ghosts here on earth. I think they are demons disguising themselves as humans. They do this to cause the exact same doubt I went through. Those who doubt the Bible are in danger of living the rest of their lives in death. I also believe that since all of the earth is made up of energy, the energy of humans can be stored and "replayed" over again in what could be called "residual haunts", and this could be regarded as another form of ghost.

Loneliness is the most powerful of all the emotions. When we lose someone, we want to be able to communicate with them. This is a way of avoiding the emotional pain of loneliness. What a better opportunity could there be for the devil to cast doubt into your mind than when you are lonely?

In my art series *Demon vs. Angel* from *Dreams, Nightmares, Fears and Fantasy Collection: Volume 1*, you will see this very event replayed in art form.

The demon enters the room through the closet as it looks for its victim. The angel looks vigilant ready to tackle and defeat the beast. They meet up, and the holy light emulates from the angel, as she is given the power from God to defeat the beast and overpower it. She then sucks the demon into a mirror sending it back to hell, trapped forever.

The power struggle you see the angel and demon take part in, is the sort of fight I had with the shadow demon, and when I touched the spirit with the Bible, it sucked the entity back to Hell. In my art, the mirror is the same personification of that moment. Then, the angel gives a sigh of relief, knowing tranquility is brought back into the home.

From this moment on, I was never scared of the paranormal again, nor am I scared of demonic entities. In fact, there isn't much that does scare me… well except spiders and clowns, but those are other stories to be told later.

I have since been known to challenge entities, antagonize them and try to get them to make contact; something that other paranormal investigators tend to shy away from.

The demon enters the house through the closet.

And he makes his way through the house.

An angel stands guard over the home.

She senses danger and attempts to seek it out.

The demon enters the bedroom.

And he is confronted by the angel.

The Angel and Demon confront each other.

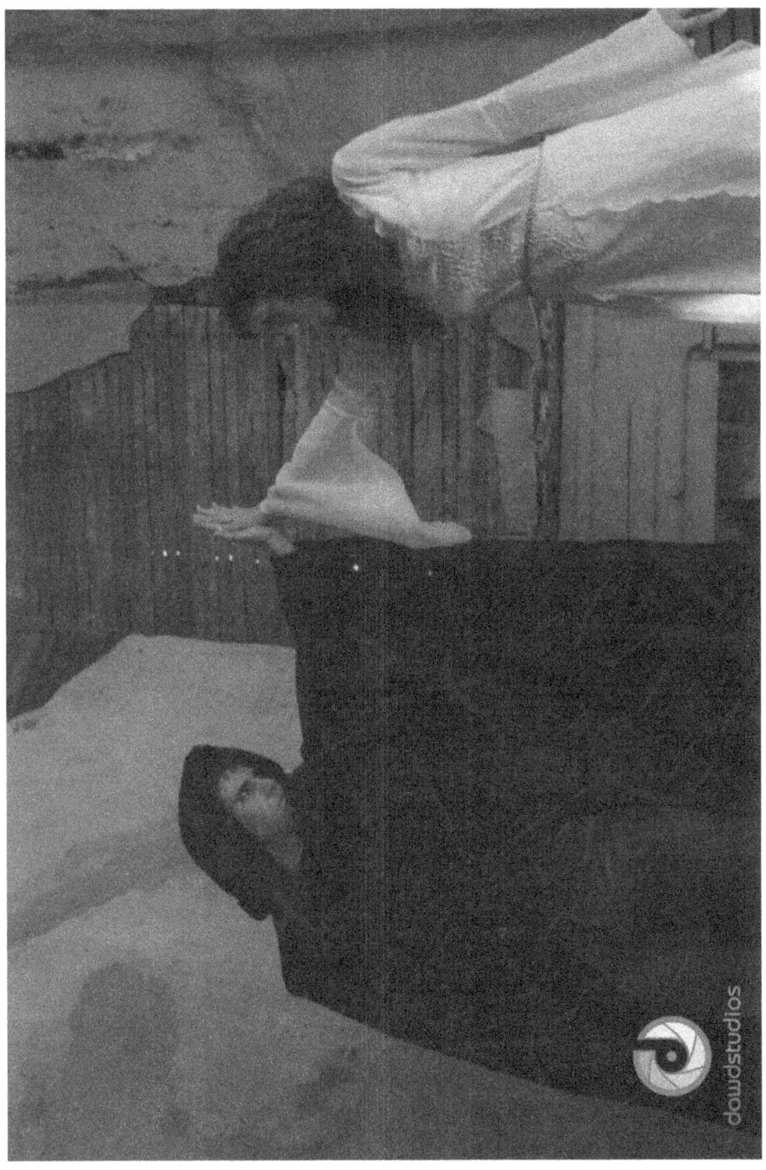

They lock in a battle of strength, Good vs. Evil.

God's Light and Power begins to shine in the Angel.

The smaller angel then starts to overpower the beast.

As she shines God's Holiness in its face, the beast turns.

dowdstudios

The Glory of God is too much for the demon who cowers before the Almighty God.

The demon surrenders.

This is symbolic of the moment I placed the bible on the demon, sending it to Hell. In this depiction, the bible is represented by a mirror.

The demon is trapped in the mirror.

Chapter 9 – I Meet a Girl in a Dream

After I fought with the demon and cast it out, my life changed radically. I noticed that I could see life through someone else's eyes and feel someone else's emotions. I could literally turn myself into that person if I wanted to, as if I were a demon taking possession of someone. This was no dream, because I was completely awake and fully conscious. I had never before seen life as someone else through my own eyes, and that really freaked me out.

For as long as I can remember, I had known something was wrong with me or "missing" and once in a while this type of out of body experience would happen to me; but only now I could do it on demand. I really thought I was possessed and that my fight to remove the demon had only succeeded in taking the evil entity out of the house and bringing it into me.

This has never gone away. I can still see life as someone else through my eyes. The big difference is that now it makes complete sense to me and I understand it.

I never saw the demon again, but, three months later, another strange incident transpired. It didn't come in the form of a spirit. This time, it came in the form of a beautiful dream.

The dream was far from being a nightmare. In fact, it was probably one of the best dreams I ever had. Unlike my past nightmares that reoccurred over and over again, this was a one-time dream. It made me feel so good that I begged for it to return, but once the last instance of the dream occurred, it never again came back. Like my dream of being buried alive, this one was so real and elicited so many emotions in me, it was hard to determine if it was real or just a dream; and honestly to this day I still don't know if it was real or not.

The dream went like this.....

The Dream I Had About a Young Girl

One morning before school, I get up out of bed and go to wash up, as I do every day. I wash my hair because it is always greasy, even if I wash it the night before. Then I brush my teeth and comb my hair.

There is a vanity in the bathroom that holds the sink. There is only one sink, and right above it is a mirror that extends from the countertop all the way to the ceiling.

I do not look at myself as I brush my teeth. I always tilt my head down because it helps to avoid any gag reflexes. I look up occasionally, but this one time when I glance up, I am caught off guard. I hear a faint giggle that makes me look up. It isn't my brother or my parents. It is a young girl. Since I don't have any sisters and my mother is the only female in the house, this is very strange.

There in the mirror is a beautiful brown-haired girl. She has shoulder length hair, a heart-shaped face, big blue eyes, and a wonderful smile.

I spit out my toothpaste and rinse fast, and then I quickly look up again to see if I am imagining this girl. When I look up, she is still there, and she's still giggling.

Out of sheer shock, I jump back away from the sink and slam against the wall. I say: "Who are you, and why are you laughing?"

She replies: "Don't worry. I'm not going to hurt you, but I'm laughing because you're in your underwear."

I look down and see that she is right. I grab a towel from the towel rack in front of the toilet and wrap it around me as quickly as I can.

The girl says: "I don't know why you're bothering to do that. It's not like I didn't see you already."

She is still giggling. My face is beet red, but I compose myself and get up close to the mirror for a better look.

I'm thinking: "It's a portal I can pass through to another world, just like the *Hug-A-Bunch* story from the 1980's." I start to put my hand on the mirror to see if I can poke at her nose. I'm surprised that my hand doesn't go through the mirror.

She says: "Um, you're in my personal bubble."

I quickly pull my finger down and apologize.

She says: "Do you take everything so seriously? Geesh, I was just joking with you."

I reply: "I'm jumpy because it's not every day a girl shows up in my fricking mirror. I'm just defensive, that's all. Anyway, my name is Jason. What's yours?"

She replies: "You may call me Jenna, but over here we have no names."

I ask: "How did you get in the mirror?"

Jenna replies: "Well, I guess I made my mother mad or something and one day she cast a spell on me which sent me into this mirror. I don't know what I did to her, but I've been in here ever since."

I say: "That's sad...did you live here before?"

Jenna answers: "Yes, I was here for a while. My family moved out right before you moved in."

I ask curiously: "How can we get you out?"

Jenna replies: "There is no way. I wish there was because I am really bored over here. I'm looking for friends, but there are not many my age."

I tell Jenna: "So why are you coming to the mirror now? I mean, I've been here so long and have never seen you before."

Jenna says: "Yes and no. I've shown myself to you, but you just never paid attention."

I say to her: "You weren't that demon I just fought were you?"

Jenna says: “No, that was a bad situation. I was scared for you. I've seen it before, but I tried to stay away from it. I don't know what possessed you to take it on, but you took a big risk.”

I say: “So why me? What made you show yourself to me?”

Jenna says: “Don't flatter yourself, but you are a bit more special than most. I feel a good connection with you, so I thought I would reach out.”

I feel honored, and I say: “A connection?”

Jenna replies: “Yeah, a connection. I don't know what it is, but I really think by showing myself to you, good things will happen.”

I’m not about to argue. I’m just trying to comprehend what is going on.

I ask Jenna: “What did your parents do with your belongings?”

She replies: “They took some of my most prized stuff and placed it in a hole under that sink, to keep it close but out of sight. The rest they gave away.”

I immediately open the cabinet under the sink and find a makeshift floor to the vanity. I pull it up to see the hole she was talking about. I reach in and pull out her shoes, a shirt, a pair of jeans, a hair tie and a gold bracelet.

I say: “Hey I found your stuff!”

I smell her shirt, and it still smells like her, despite it having been inside a dark, damp sink basin for years.

She exclaims: “You did!”

I reply: “Yes I did.”

I show her the things I found. A tear runs down her cheek, especially when she sees the bracelet. She says: “That bracelet was given to me by my father. He left and forgot about me.”

I reached up to the mirror to wipe the tears from her cheek, but I hit the mirror instead.

She says: “Please, keep those items with you and don't let anyone see them.” I agree to do that.

I say: “Well, I have to get ready for school. Will I see you around?”

Jenna says: “Yes, of course. Anytime you need me, just call my name while you’re standing at this mirror.” Then, she disappears.

I take her clothes and put them in my room for safe keeping. After she leaves, I have this strange connection to her. I understand what she means about a connection. It is an instant love, but not the sort of love a boy would have for a girl, but rather a love for a great friend or a sister.

I go to school, but I can’t concentrate at school. All I think of is Jenna. I am addicted to her.

I must find a way to get her out of that mirror. I’m thinking: “That’s no life for her. She needs to be loved, to be a real child; and one day an adult.”

I have no answer about getting her out of the mirror, but we form an inseparable bond. She is my best friend, and I’m sure that I am her best friend. With her, I can do anything.

I find that I’m able to conjure her up whenever I want to. The next time I see her, I ask her a quick question: “This mirror keeps you trapped from the real world, and you can't escape right?”

Jenna answers: “Right.”

I say: “So that brings me to my next question... can you appear in any mirror?”

She replies: “Well, I guess so… yes. Why?”

I say: “No reason, just asking.”

I have a plan. I stop by at a gift shop and purchase a small wallet-size mirror with a blue rubber case that it slips into. This is an odd purchase for me to make because I do not like looking at myself in any mirror.

I'm thinking that if Jenna could appear in any mirror, this small pocket mirror would allow me to take her anywhere and show her the world, despite being trapped. This is a way to "break the curse" by finding a loophole.

I conjure up Jenna. She appears and gives me a big smile. She says: "Hey, sweetie! What's going on? You look excited."

I say: "I got this pocket mirror. See if you can appear in it".

She smiles and nods. She knows what I'm getting at. Then, I look down at the mirror. I'm scared because I do not want to fail, so I close my eyes tightly while I wait. Finally I hear her say: "Look." I look down at the mirror in my hand and there she is!

All I can say is: "SWEET!"

She is smiling from ear to ear. I tell her: "Now I can take you and show you the world, and you will always be by my side."

From that point on, I carry that mirror everywhere, and I mean everywhere. I keep the sleeve on the mirror, but I take it out of the sleeve when I am sitting in class during school so she can learn too. I take her everywhere I go, and we talk every night when I am in bed.

Finally, Jenna says to me one night: "You are amazing. I am so glad the world has the chance to experience you."

And then… I woke up.

I would have this dream… basically the same dream, but different scenarios and adventures… for the next few weeks until one day it was over. It was back to real life for me. I never had that dream again, but I sure wish I did. The dream had started to feel like it was a part of my daily life.

Like I said, I couldn't tell if that dream was real or just a figment of my subconscious imagination but once the dream was over for good, I had to find out just how real it was. I ran into the bathroom and checked under the sink. I moved some of the shelf paper at the bottom… and I discovered a large hole. NO LIE… it was there.

I reached my hand in and *de ja vu* took over. I didn't find clothes, but I did find a friendship bracelet. I knew that it didn't belong to anyone that was exiled into a mirror, but it was pretty cool to have. I still have that bracelet, and I will always cherish it as a reminder of the most beautiful dream I ever had.

That dream was so amazing and realistic. Before I had the dream, I didn't know the bottom of the vanity was lined in shelf paper. How would I have known there was a hole in there? How could anyone explain why the shelf paper looked real? To this day, I still have no explanation for this. I had no idea who Jenna was, but I knew I had to find out… somehow… no matter how long it took.

Chapter 10 – School Daze

Trouble began for me from the very first day I started school in Florida. I was supposed to be in sixth grade, but they pushed me back into fifth grade even though I had been making straight A's in Connecticut. It had nothing to do with lack of academic achievement. It was all because I was born on November 1st, which was past the cutoff date.

On my very first day in fifth grade, in 1990, the teacher gave a science test. The teacher said to me: "Look, Jason, I don't know how far along you are or what you know, so I'm not going to hold it against you, unless you do really well. If you don't do well, don't worry about it. It will just give me an idea of where you are at."

When I came back to school the next day, the teacher said to the class: "I am sooo disappointed with everybody in this class. The highest grade in this class on this test was a C… except for one person. She walked over to me and said: "He got a hundred percent, plus all the bonus questions."

This was not a good move by the teacher. It set me up as being the kid everyone should compare themselves too: The new guy who had never done the work and still scored one hundred percent. All of the other students knew that I hadn't even picked up the textbook. It was as if the teacher had said to them: "You guys have been studying for three weeks and you still can't get it right."

I didn't have to study until my sophomore year at Land O'Lakes High School. That was when my classes finally reached the level of work I had been doing during my sixth grade year in Connecticut. My first teacher in Florida had good intentions, but the road to Hell is paved with good intentions. It really caused me terrible problems. She was embarrassed as well. She must have thought: "Here's a kid who hasn't set foot in this school before, and he aced a test on stuff he shouldn't have known." In my honest opinion, she projected her failure as a teacher onto me rather than cope with her embarrassment. She didn't realize that I was really in sixth grade and that the textbook she was using was the equivalent of my fourth grade science book in Connecticut. Back there, I was already learning about things five times more advanced than what they were doing down in Florida. For me, it was like nothing. It's not that I am smarter or better than any of the kids here, it was just a case how education differs in the different regions of the country.

Back at the Lutheran school in Connecticut, I had to learn the entire Lutheran Small Catechism, which included all the creeds, before I was in second grade. We not only had to learn each commandment, we also had to completely understand its meaning. We were tested once a week, sometimes two or three times a week because we had to have it all done by the end of the school year. I memorized The Large Catechism in fifth and sixth grade, and I still have most of that memorized.

My first day in a Florida school was a preview of future problems. I was bullied all the time. In fact, I'm surprised I'm not as vindictive as perhaps I should be. Some kids devised an instrument to torture me with. They would take a pencil with an eraser at one end, remove the rubber eraser from the metal used to attach it to the pencil and then push the metal together to make a sharp edge. My ears stuck out and provided attractive targets. The bullies would use their pencils with sharp edges to "whap" my ear lobe from behind. One time, a blow from a bully's pencil sliced my ear lobe. It didn't cut it off entirely. It was only partially severed and was flopping around while I bled profusely.

I had been told in my karate training that karate should be used as a defense, and not as offense. Karate is much more than a sport; it is a way of life. It teaches that it is better to use your brain than your brawn. I truly believe that.

For that very reason, it would have been considered an act of aggression… or "offense"… if I had retaliated against the bully who had nearly sliced my ear lobe off. According to the principles of karate, I could justify using my defensive skills only in the case of stopping an attack. If I did not know an attack was coming, I would have to show resilience in bouncing back from whatever injury I might suffer. You must also be able to control your actions, because you can kill people with force; especially the trained force I learned.

In the case of the bully who nearly removed my ear lobe, I simply turned around and said to him: "It takes an idiot to attack someone from behind. It takes a true soul to forgive."

By doing that, he never hurt me again because I had not given him what he needed… which was the ability to intimidate me. I had learned an extreme form of restraint from karate that allowed me to stop a bully without using one ounce of force. Instead, I defeated him with my brain. My ear would heal.

There were times, though, when a dose of brawn, judiciously used, was needed to remedy a situation. On another occasion, a girl named Sherry, who was a friend of mine, was working with me in a biology lab. We were dissecting frogs. A bully came up behind me and began rubbing the back of my head saying: "How about this, lover boy?" He began rubbing my ears and giving me "wet willies" (He would lick the tip of his little finger, and then he would stick it into my ear.). I said: "Stop, dude."

Sherry was a tough cookie, the type who wouldn't let anybody pick on her. I had been friends with her since sixth grade. This was toward the end of my freshman year. The older kid was 16 years old at the time. He wouldn't let up and he said to her: "Ooh, do you like lovin' him?"

She said: "No, stop!!"

We were at the point of getting fed up. Just then, the bully viciously snapped a rubber band on her leg in such a way that it managed to split her skin open.

I hollered: "YOU S.O.B.!!" but I didn't use as nice a word.

I then took my dissecting scalpel and sliced open the front of his shirt… a gorgeous nylon shirt. I knew what I was doing and I made sure not to break the skin when I slashed his shirt. He immediately played the "victim card" by running to a teacher and telling them what I had done.

The teacher said: "I know Jason too well. You must have done some pretty nasty stuff for him to do that to you. I've never known him to be violent about anything." The teacher sided with me because of the good reputation I had among the faculty. The bully wound up getting suspended for a week. I have to also mention that the teacher reprimanded me for using such a dangerous object against him, but she knew the bully was violent, and that I was in full control of what I was doing. I did get into a bit of trouble, but not nearly as much as the bully did.

The kids who tried to pick on me were mostly rednecks. They were probably having their own issues about fitting in. I could empathize with them, and I understood what they were going through. They were really country here then here comes a Yankee boy trying to live with and get along with them. I was the new kid on the totem pole, but not necessarily the low man. I was proud of myself as everyone should be, but the teacher had unwittingly made a target of me because of the science test years ago. Most of the kids in the Land O'Lakes area back then did not like northerners because their parents had little use for them. You have to remember that this was in the early 1990's. Land O'Lakes has grown up a bit since then.

I had a New England accent, I stood out, and the girls liked it. The boys hated me, though, because their girls stayed with me instead of them. And they really shouldn't have worried because I didn't go out with any of the girls. Where I came from, dating was taboo until you were old enough and had the means to drive. Watching kids in their early teens dating blew my mind. I couldn't believe the schools allowed it. Maybe that was another why the girls liked me so much. I didn't want to date them; I just wanted to be their friend.

When I first arrived in Florida, kids used to come around me and make me talk because I had an accent which they found hilarious; but I really didn't know what was going on. It proved to be my good fortune when a kid named Paul Knox came into my life.

Paul was born in Scotland had a Scottish accent which he could turn on and off. He picked up on what the other kids were doing to me, and he walked over to them and said in his Scottish accent: "If you're gonna pick on him and make him do that, then I don't need to be your friend either." They stopped them in their tracks.

I said to Paul: "What are you talking about?"

He replied: "Dude, you have an accent. And they're making you talk as a way of picking on you."

So, that was how we became really good friends

Both Paul and his twin sister were born in Scotland. You had to listen to him to hear any accent because he was very young when he moved here, but he still had one.

Paul's friendship helped a great deal, but didn't really solve the problem. I was being bullied so much because of my accent that it got to the point where my school insisted I take a speech therapy class in hopes of resolving the issue. Their method solved nothing and actually led to further difficulty for me. As a result of all that therapy, I stutter because I have to think about what I'm about to say in order to assure that I do not say it with a New England accent. In their concern over the possibilities of my being seriously hurt, they wound up punishing the victim. And let it known that when I become angry enough… the accent returns!

Bully problems were not the only adversity I encountered in high school. There was the time one of my teachers created a mess for me by overreacting.

I was an 18-year-old junior at the time. It all started when one of my teachers was trying to make the point that: "Everything has a meaning in literature." I didn't agree with that statement and I tried to disprove it by writing something which was nothing but meaningless gibberish and turned it into that teacher. It was all intended as harmless fun.

The next thing I know, I was sitting in my American History class when some cops came in, threw me to the floor, handcuffed me and took me down to the guidance counselor. They thought I was going to kill myself.

I told them: "I'm not going to kill myself. I don't WANT to kill myself. What would make you think that?" They produced the silly gibberish I had written as evidence. That was their only proof of my intention to commit suicide. Thankfully, it all got straightened out before I was taken to a mental health facility.

I always had a gift of writing. I won a "Pride in Writing" award two years in a row… in 1990 and 1991… for all of Pasco County, Florida.

After the teacher overreacted and got me in trouble, though, I completely stopped writing. I was so traumatized that it set me back. The first "real" or "serious" thing I wrote was a song called "Wings", but that was years later when my friend committed suicide in 2006.

When I was taken to the guidance counselor in handcuffs back in 1997, I begged them, trying to convince them that I was not going to kill myself. My intention was to prove to this lady that every piece of writing does not have to have a meaning. You don't always have to have a meaning to write something… it could just be for fun. I proved my point, but it was a case of: "Don't ask for what you wish for because sometimes you may be shocked when your wish is granted."

As the end of high school years approached, I had to take the usual standardized tests. I got a perfect score on my English SAT's. I screwed the Math up tremendously, but… oh well!

I took advanced placement classes in senior year, in addition to taking nothing but honors classes in both my junior and senior years. I actually had far more credits than I needed to graduate, since I had been taking courses at Pasco/Hillsborough Community College at night. I was in high school, enrolled in a community college and working, all at the same time. I did what I needed to do, and I focused on school.

I held several part time jobs through high school and college. In fact, a part-time security gig for Tampa Bay Lightning hockey games wound up changing my life. That was how I met my wife Fran.

Fran's mom worked at the Ice Palace. Fran was looking for something to do that was a way of making money, but was also fun. So, her mom got her working as a ticket taker at the arena.

After Fran started working there, her mom actually set us up for a date; and then she hated every bit of it. Her mom hated me for the longest time, and it started from the very first time Fran and I went out. Isn't that ironic?? It took Fran's mom years, but she finally got over it.

It all stemmed from the fact that Fran has five other siblings, and she's the youngest in the family. Most of her siblings married, but later divorced. That hit Fran's mother hard. As a result, she became very protective of Fran. She didn't want to see her baby daughter go through the heartache of divorce.

A difference in our religions also came into play. Fran is of German, Irish, Dutch and Polish descent, and her family members are staunch Catholics. As a result, her mother did not like the fact that I was Lutheran.

In addition, her mom was always worried that I was going to take over the family's estate. I'm not like that, and I really could care less. Fran finally convinced her mom when she said: "If anything happened to our parents, I would be making out better than him."

They basically excommunicated her and disowned her for a while, but in her family, everybody has been disowned and brought back at least two or three times. My wife and I have shared interests. For instance, both Fran and I love sports.

Unlike what I experienced with my mother-in-law, my mom loved Fran from the minute she met her. There have never been any problems between them that I ever saw, and my wife and my mom enjoy a great relationship.

In the end, love conquered all. Fran and I married in July, 2000.

"Death To Yesterday"

Chapter 11 - Death to Yesterday

In May 2006, I was looking for models to work with in order to expand my portfolio. I ran across a female model named Orieas, who was a fashion model in the Tampa Bay area and had a look about her that made her a terrific candidate for a photo shoot. So, I clicked on her official website and it took me to MySpace.

I opened a MySpace account just so I could e-mail Orieas. I never got a response, but really it wasn't a big deal. An unintended consequence of my opening the MySpace account turned out to be far bigger. Old friends from school found me on that social network site and requested that I link them to my page as "friends".

That sparked my "social networking" rage. I became very excited about the prospects of seeing and talking to people I haven't heard from in nine years! After going through all the ones who had found me, I decided to search for everyone I had known and see if they had a MySpace profile. One person I was particularly interested in was my dear friend… a friend whom I considered my "best friend of all"… Paul Knox.

Paul was always full of laughs, so when I searched his name, I not only found it; I also found a picture of the comedian "Borat" which he was using for his profile picture. This may sound silly, but at that time, I didn't know who Borat was. My initial reaction was: "Is that Paul?" Now that I'm familiar with Borat, I have to admit that my old friend kind of resembled the comedic character a bit and it wouldn't surprise me if he dressed up like him. Anyhow, I "friend requested" him and sent him the following message:

"Hi, I don't know if you remember me, but I hope you do. It's been like 9 years since we talked and that is something I should not have let happen; however this is Jason Dowd. I hope this is Paul Knox, but from the picture I can't tell and I can't see the rest of your profile. If it is Paul, please write back. I really miss you and I hope we can get together and catch up."

A few days later, I received a response from him which read:

"Yup the one and only, how are you doing brother. It's been way too long for sure. We should get together and catch up."

I was elated to say the least! I quickly replied to him: "Yes, let's get together and catch up. I have so much to tell you. Let me know a place and time." That was on May 30th, 2006.

A few days went by, and I didn't hear anything. So, I wrote Paul and again asked for a meet up. Once again, there was no response.

It's now June 5th, and I still had not heard from Paul. I didn't see any activity on his MySpace wall, so I e-mailed him once again, asking if he was okay. I also wrote that if he wasn't okay, I would be more than happy to help him out.

The next day, June 6th, 2006, I saw a post on my friend's MySpace wall saying: "Paul is dead."

My heart sank. I thought: "What a rotten, horrible prank to pull." So, I went to the funeral home's website to confirm what I had seen on MySpace post. There was Paul's face under his obituary!

Paul was like a brother to me, and the thought of him passing away so young made me sick to my stomach. We went way back. He had brought me my homework when I was severely sick for weeks with chicken pox. We chased girls together; and we walked and rode bikes almost every day, covering the entire sub division of Lake Padgett East. He helped me through my parents' divorce and stood up for me when other kids picked on me in fifth grade.

Instantly the thoughts "could of, would of, should of" ran through my mind. Had I known he was depressed, I could have stopped him from committing suicide. I should have sought him out sooner, and maybe his passing wouldn't have happened. I would have known how much he was hurting, had I been a better friend. Those thoughts were tearing me apart. I had failed him as a friend!

I still have his last message to me saved on my MySpace account. I hold that message dear to me. Had I known that was going to be the last thing I would ever say to him alive, I would have come up with something a lot better to say!

Back when we graduated from high school, Paul thought I was going to MIT or Virginia Tech. I was supposed to go to Virginia Tech after graduation, but I was denied a scholarship due to affirmative action; so I never left the state. The night of our graduation, Paul said to me: "We'll see each other again before 10 years go by, if not you'll have to come back for the reunion!"

I made one mistake that night. I didn't get his phone number. I assumed that, since he was so smart, he would be going off to college. He didn't and like me, he never left Land O Lakes.

I would drive by his mom's house in Lake Padgett East all the time and remember the good moments we shared together (way before his death), yet I never stopped in. I was always afraid his mom may have moved away and some stranger would answer the door. Now that I look back on it, where could I have gotten such a crazy idea?

I often ask myself: "With all my abilities and forewarnings that come to me and all my psychic abilities… why didn't they take hold for this?" The only answer I can come up with is that they did… I did seek him out, after all… but it was a day late and a dollar short. Sure, I didn't realize what I had at the time, but I still wonder why those instincts didn't kick in.

At the funeral, I was reunited with my friend for the first time in nine years. It was held nine years to the day from our graduation, June 6, 2006. Paul was right. We would get together within ten years, but I never imagined it would happen like this.

There was his lifeless body, grey from carbon monoxide poisoning; a body once filled with life and laughter and compassion now lifeless and sick. It was all too surreal. Unlike my grandmother Ama, Paul didn't look real in his casket.

I think the thing that got me the most was watching a little girl around the age of nine go up to the casket and fix Paul's hair. She was crying, and that choked me up a bit. She returned to the seat next to his mom, Carolyn. Before the ceremony started, I went over to give my condolences to his mom.

I said: "Hi Carolyn, I don't know if you remember me at all, but your son was one of my best friends in middle school and high school." She shook her head and in a Scottish brogue said: "No, I'm sorry I don't remember. I am glad you came though."

I talked with her for a few moments, and she introduced me to the little girl who was fixing Paul's hair. His mom said: "I want you to meet Nellie. Her name is Janelle, but we call her Nellie. She is Paul's daughter."

My heart sank even more. What I saw before me was a bright eyed, beautiful little girl that he left behind. I knew he had to be suffering horribly to leave someone like her behind, but I knew he would have taken measures to insure she was safe and taken care of. I knew Carolyn, too, and that was not going to be a problem.

After that incident I rekindled my friendship with the family. I adore his mom and family, and just love his daughter to death. She is so special and I am so proud of the way she's turned out. Paul himself would be proud.

After the funeral was over and I talked with his mom, I still couldn't shake the "would of, could of, should of" thought process. She told me to stop thinking like that because it was just meant to be.

I felt really guilty about his death. To this day, I still feel like I may have been able to change the outcome, if only I had kept in touch with him. It was a case of my taking a friendship for granted, and I will never do that again.

Despite the kind words, I started to get really depressed about his death. I really have never been the same since the funeral. I did start to get a reoccurring image that haunted my dreams, but it wasn't scary.

The image is of a person mourning over a grave stone, completely forlorn and depressed over their loss, yet standing behind them with a comforting hand on their shoulder is a ghostly image of that person. They aren't dead; in fact they are very much alive as they cry over the grave. It took me a little while to understand the meaning of that dream. It is an image of Paul, and he's trying to comfort me.

I didn't understand why, but I had to take the image and make it into a photograph. It was only after I shot the photograph that I understood the meaning of that dream. The photograph was the very first photo of my *Dreams, Nightmares, Fears and Fantasy* collection. The photo would also end up on display in Hong Kong, China and San Diego, California.

The meaning is beautiful and it goes something like this:

The lady mourning over the grave is very much alive. She is very distraught over what she lost. Yet behind her is a spiritual image of her. The ghostly image is calm, happy and at peace. She places her hand on the mourner's shoulder to comfort her.

The ghost of the mourning lady represents "Yesterday". It's her past. It's there to comfort her, showing her that what happened yesterday is done. You can't change the past, but the past is always with you in memory and lives in your heart and mind. It's there to bring a smile back to your face and it's something nobody can take from you. Living in the past and crying over the past is wasteful. You should, instead, learn from your experiences and mistakes and live for today, in order to make tomorrow a better future for yourself.

Paul was telling me to stop crying over spilled milk. He is fine, in fact better than ever. He doesn't hurt anymore, he can still watch over and protect Nellie and his family, and he can still be with me when I need a friend. I was not being productive by being angry at myself over what happened.

In fact, Paul helped me start the art series that has taken the world by storm. I only wish I had the chance to tell him to his face while he was on earth how much he meant to me, and that he was my best friend. I will never have that chance, but at least I know he knows.

A Dime for your Thoughts

I've seen Paul a lot since his death. He's come to me in dreams; he's even showed himself to me in spirit. We talk all the time and it's a wonderful experience.

Shortly after his death, his mom started to tell me she would find dimes everywhere. This was very odd because she usually paid for her purchases with a credit card, so change should have been scarce in her house. I do the same thing; and change is a rarity around my home.

Anyway, Carolyn read somewhere that spirits sometimes leave you little things to remind you of them and let you know they are there. For Paul, that was leaving dimes.

She would often find a dime lying on the floor while vacuuming. She would find dimes in her bed and in places you don't normally find change lying around.

After she told me about it, the same thing started happening to me. I remember two instances very profoundly.

The first one happened durring a from hell at my job. My boss was ripping into me, and I just couldn't take the abuse anymore.

I started to get really angry over the littlest things. Then I got another scathing e-mail from my boss.

I cracked. I began to pound on my computer's keys while responding to him. Suddenly, I felt something strange under my hand. I lifted my palm up from the keyboard to find a dime. I had been typing for hours, hardly ever taking my hand off the keyboard, so how could a dime appear? There hadn't been any change on the computer table because I never have any change.

I looked at the date on the coin, and it was 1997… the year I graduated from high school. The dime was a message from Paul saying: "TAKE A CHILL PILL DUDE!"

Another incident took place right before a stressful weekend. It was the last Friday in October, and it was Halloween. I was to shoot two weddings that weekend, one on my birthday in Ft. Meyers and one on Sunday, November 2nd for a dear friend of mine. On that particular Sunday, the Patriots (my favorite football team) were playing the Colts in Indianapolis. Both had 9-0 records and were playing for a shot at remaining undefeated in the NFL. I had a lot riding on my shoulders that weekend.

Fran and I decided to celebrate my birthday by going out for dinner on Halloween. We went to Chili's in Land O'Lakes. After we parked our car, I got out of the vehicle and looked down at my feet. There was a shiny dime!

I picked it up and the year on the coin was 2006, the year Paul died. The dime had a unique gouge on it that covered Eisenhower's eye, something that made it stand out. I put it in my pocket and carried it around with me the whole weekend.

It must have been good luck because the wedding photos went splendidly, and the Patriots won against Indianapolis. That was the year they would go 16-0 and finish with an 18-1 record, losing only in the Super Bowl.

That dime was precious to me. I kept that dime and took it everywhere I went. One night while we were in Brooksville ghost hunting, Fran and I stopped for a late night snack at a

McDonald's on our way home. I paid with cash, which was unusual for me, and I unwittingly spent my dime from Paul. I was devastated to say the least.

In 2009, I went to a store in Land O Lakes that was 35 miles from the McDonalds where I had spent the dime. I paid cash for the item which again was odd, since I normally pay by credit card, and in among the change was the 2006 dime with that gouge down the front covering the same eye on Eisenhower. I couldn't believe it, my dime was back and I still have it today… and I will guard it like the most precious stone in the world.

The theory behind these objects, especially coins, is that the date usually means something. It's a year when something major happened to you with that departed person or to them or strictly to you. I usually get dimes from Paul with the year 1990, when we met, 1993, when we had one of our best summers together, 1997, when we graduated, and 2006, the year he died.

The lesson to be learned from this is: Keep your eyes open for signs; you never know where they will appear and how they will be given. You may completely overlook the signs; as I did for far too long. If you overlook them, you will regret how much you missed.

Chapter 12 – Death Defied

In November, 2009, I had a near death experience… well not just near death, I actually died. I felt so empty, so confused and abused that I couldn't live anymore. It was football season, so I put on my New England Patriots football jersey, long pants and put on a shirt underneath the jersey.

Since I was upset, I decided to go cool off with a car ride. I guess my anger caused my blood sugar to drop because I never made it out of the parking lot. My blood sugar just crashed right there on the spot, and I was really "86ed" for a while. As I got into the car, I started feeling really woozy. I thought: "Oh, I don't feel good at all!" I got to the point where I was really tired, and then I passed out.

I am vulnerable to low blood sugar issues. Generally, my sugar is between 40 and 80. After drinking two large sodas, it will be at 80, when it should be well over 400. All while this was going on, Fran had been watching me through the front window of our home, but she thought I just needed to blow off some steam, so she let me be.

I had on jeans, shoes, plus a New England Patriots jersey (which was made of nylon and held in sweat). The car was sweltering hot and I foolishly locked the doors when I got in. When my blood sugar crashed, I stopped functioning properly. The sun was beating right down on my car. It must have been 82 degrees outside so inside the car it was like 115 degrees, I was slowly cooking to death and I couldn't do anything to fix it.

I couldn't move well, but my mind was functioning. I saw my life flash before my face. Since I was already angry, I thought that if I was gone, people would see what they were missing. Maybe they would stop bullying others after learning what they did to me.

After 25 minutes of broiling heat, I started to get really tired, and I eventually passed out. The doors were locked, the windows were rolled up and all keys to my car were on my belt loop. At that moment, I fell asleep... and I died.

I was taken to a light, a light I will never forget. It wasn't scary. It was beautiful and so serene. As I moved closer to the light, I saw a divide; the bright white light on one side and complete darkness on the other.

On the light side, there was true harmony, love and compassion. There were no wants, no hunger… just pure bliss. It was a place I would want to live in forever.

On the other side was sheer black, so black that it made the night look like midday. The horror on that side would chill anyone to the bone. The crying and the agony were fierce. What was worse, there was a complete lack of love. Try to comprehend that. It is almost too difficult to do so. On earth, we have a balance of good and evil. We see people that don't love, yet we are still capable of loving if we want to. But in the dark place, you CANNOT LOVE. There is only hate, despair and agony. Imagine a world without love!

I saw Heaven and I saw Hell. I was standing in the middle. I realized that life is a “balancing act”. We live among those two worlds, and yes there is evil on the earth, yet many of us try to overlook it and/or live it and justify it as being right.

We all want peace on earth, but as long as there is a shred of evil the size of a grain of salt on the earth, this will never be accomplished until Jesus comes again. World Peace, hunger, no more poverty, all that… won't happen until He comes again.

I knew Heaven and Hell existed, and I knew my Redeemer truly lived. My religion was solidified, yet I didn't need to see this to believe it, I already believed.

Then in a flash, I was being pulled back to my body. I honestly can say that I didn't want to go. I wanted to be with the Lord. I heard a voice say: “You are not supposed to be here yet. You must go back. You have so much left to do.”

I woke up outside of my car. The doors were still locked, the windows were rolled up tight and there was nobody around. No one could have gotten to me without shattering the glass, which didn't happen.

It was a miracle. There is a purpose for everything that happens. I was spared because I was given the task of showing the balance of good and evil on earth. I was to show that God's mercy will balance the bad and destroy evil upon his return and save those who have been redeemed and believe in Jesus. He let me go so that, through my experience, I would understand the balance of good and evil and portray it in my art work. And the art work started to roll out of me later that month.

Now, I truly know what it is like to die. I am not afraid of death anymore. What I fear is leaving everyone here on earth behind. My period of epiphany was not over, however. One year later, I would make another amazing discovery.

Chapter 13 - DOUBLE TROUBLE

It was now 2010. I was 31 years old and I couldn't stop thinking about how strange my life actually was. I had been able to see ghosts more and more. I could sense people's energy and I found that I have psychic abilities. I also realized I could see my life through someone else's eyes in my own body. I never quite lost what I had as a child by growing up. If anything, it intensified.

Strangely enough, all the way through school, girls told me they didn't want me as a boyfriend, because it was like dating their best friend or sister. Women could talk to me about anything, private things, and have no reservation about it. I didn't mind that, either. I also found out I got along better with females and could relate to them better than I could with guys.

None of this made sense. I always distanced myself away from people in school for fear they would see what I could. I didn't want anyone to know what was going on in my life.

Like I said, I always knew something was missing, I just didn't know what that was. I battled unpredictable bouts of depression, a feeling of being separated from someone very close to me without having any idea of who they were. Other strange phenomenon had occurred. It wasn't until 2010 that everything made sense.

In 2009, I started work on my series *Dreams, Nightmares, Fears and Fantasy*. The photographic series helped me deal with these feelings, while at the same time bringing to life some of my strange dreams. One of which was me being buried alive, the dream I had since I was six. I called that series *Trapped, But Not Dead*. On the other hand, a dream of mine that played very vividly was *Death to Yesterday*... a dream that surfaced after my best friend Paul committed suicide in 2006. It was a dream that told me: "Don't worry about or mourn for yesterday. Live for today and take the memories of yesterday with you. You are not living if you are mourning the past."

My photographic series contains vivid pictures of dreams, visions and more that I have had over the last few years, including my encounters with the paranormal. The *Demon vs. Angel* series depicts the night I fought the demon in my old house on Canterbury Drive in Land O'Lakes, Florida.

Anyway, my mother had a Tarot card reading done for her by a friend. The reading was very accurate, and Mom told me how impressive it was. So, I said to her: "Just for fun, ask your friend if she'll do one for me." I was in a bad position at the time and I thought a Tarot card reading might shine some light on the situation.

I gave my mom's friend a compact flash card I made most of my art series with, so that she would have a good vision of me. It was something I carried around a lot and something I physically portrayed my heart and soul in. If anything contained me on it, it was that compact flash card.

A few days later my mom got the reading back. Her friend gave her explicit instructions. I was to call Mom's friend that night for my reading, but before that, I was to call my mom so she could tell me something I had to know before I got my reading.

When my mom called, she told me something that took all my years of confusion and made sense out of it. The news was so powerful it would change my life forever.

She was at the dentist with my brother, and she couldn't talk long, so we had only a brief conversation. She said: "Jason, you are to call her tonight after six. However before you do, I need to tell you something. It is something you must hear from me. You are very powerful. You have extreme psychic abilities. There is one thing I need to tell you; something I never told you before. Jason, when you were born, there was another placenta. You are a twin... the Tarot reader told me about this and she asked me if I had I ever told you. I told her I had not. She said: 'You must tell him because I must tell him.'"

My mom knew that if she did not tell me about the twin she had kept secret from me and that I heard about it from her friend, then I would instantly debunk and discredit the Tarot card reader because there is no body or grave for my twin. There is no proof that my unborn twin sister ever existed.

Mom finished her statement to me by saying: "Your twin died before the second trimester, therefore there is no body; it was trashed as medical waste. You are a twin. I will tell you more later, but I have to go right now." Then she hung up.

My jaw dropped... I was actually in a state of shock. I couldn't believe what I had just heard, but I knew one thing for sure. Everything made sense.

I met with the Tarot card reader that night. When I asked her about my twin, I told her it must have been a girl. She said: "Yes, it was. You see her life through your eyes, don't you?"

It confirmed what I already had sensed. I could literally be my sister, since I can see life through her eyes whenever I want. She is very protective of me and adores me to no end.

I told the Tarot card reader about my series *Demon vs. Angel*, and that I felt compelled to portray the angel as a female because that's how I saw it in my dream… even though I was a guy I portrayed myself as a female. The rest came to pass because my sister had helped me the night I defeated the demon, since I was far too weak to tackle the beast alone. God gave my sister the ability to be my guardian angel and help me to defeat the beast.

After cleansing the demon from my home, I was made aware of my sister. What troubled me, though, was that I first thought what I felt for my sister was a sign that I had been possessed by the demon. What had really happened, though, was that a bond had been created beyond the grave between my unborn twin sister and me. It was she that I portrayed in the *Trapped, But Not Dead* series. Once again, I was driven to portray the protagonist as a female without knowing why. It was through my sister's eyes that I knew what it was like to be in a casket and die.

The best dream I ever had… meeting the girl in the mirror… turned out to be real. It was a case of my subconscious meeting my sister on the other side. An amazing connection had been established between us. That was the reason why I carried a mirror around through my school years: To assure that she could be with me.

She was cast into a mirror as a metaphor. It has been said that mirrors are so called "portals" to the other world. My unborn twin sister told me that our mother put her there. I truly believe, however, that it was nature that put her there, because she never left my mother alive. My mom never intentionally put her there. The dream was a way of telling me this so I could understand it all. My unborn twin sister has no hatred or bitterness towards my mom because she knew it was nature that caused her demise.

I also believe that she can never come out of the mirror because the dead can't come back, only Jesus did that. I do know she can use that mirror as a portal for communication. The mirror in the dream is a symbol of my heart and eyes because she lives through my heart, she sees through my eyes and I can have that inseparable bond with her forever.

The day I talked to my mom and the Tarot card reader was the day I met the other part of me. Once I met the other part of me, I no longer felt empty. I just had no idea who that girl was until 2010.

Now more than ever, I understand the bond between twins, and ironically the week before I found out I was a twin, I did a photo shoot with real twins to capture the essence of the bond they share.

It is a beautiful connection. I completely understand that it happened through no fault of my own and that for many years, I had no idea of what had taken place. She had no grave. Her placenta had been thrown out so, unless I knew there was another placenta, how would I know unless someone had told me? Yet, I always knew something was missing in my life, and that something is my unborn twin sister.

Because she is identical to me and we share the same egg; in many ways a part of me died with her. That accounts for my bouts of depression. It is she who is sad because she doesn't know what could have been, and I can feel her pain.

We are inseparable… my unborn twin sister and I… so much so that even death can't destroy the bond. She protects me. That's why I am able to walk into haunted places and not get hurt and why I show no fear. She heightens my psychic ability, and together we are as one.

I think of her as an angel, but since she is my twin, she is a part of me. Hurting me is also like hurting her. I'm sure she can feel it. There are times when I get really depressed without any apparent reason, and I believe that is because I'm feeling her pain, her isolation and depression. She wants to be with me here in this world. Most twins feel that same sort of closeness. But it fills me with hope to know that she is trying to help me.

I also believe that the hardest part for her was all those years growing up when I did not know about her. That is what really got to her more than anything. It does my heart good to know that she found a way to break through dimensions and let me know she was there. She appeared after I faced and overcame the demon. That was when my eyes were opened and a connection was made, yet I didn't know the full meaning at that time; she knew but didn't know how to tell me. I still see her in my dreams and there are also times when I physically see her in person.

I am protected because of my unborn twin sister. I have been hit by a car three times and have come away each time without a single scratch. The demon offered little resistance when I went toe to toe with it back in 1993. Spirits do not dare hurt me or mess me when I venture into haunted places. I have been in near accidents where things were about to collide with me and then at the last instant, they went in a completely opposite way; yet there I was waiting for impact.

If you want to hear a message which my unborn twin sister often tells me, it can be found it in the words of a song by Cathy Dennis titled: *Too Many Walls*. I heard this song back in the 1990's and LOVED IT. It calmed me down and I felt a very emotional connection to it, but it took me nearly ten years to learn why the song meant so much to me. The message is about the walls of death and the frustration of not being able to communicate with someone, or live with someone, especially someone who is a part of you. "Too Many Walls" is a most fitting title for the song.

When my unborn twin sister told me who she was in the dream, the walls were broken down. She schemed to find out a way to uncover the truth, and she succeeded. If she could change the ways of the world, she would be here with me as my twin sister. And even if she gave up, no one could destroy what there is between us. Through this song, my unborn twin sister talked to me and told me the truth for years, but it just a long time for me to understand her message.

Because of the song, I can also see why I had bouts of depression. The song tells of my twin sister's struggle and how upset she was that she couldn't let me know she existed. It was critical to my balance of life here on earth, and her message exposed the powers I had and helped me to make sense out of them.

The one line that stands out is: "You're so young is all they can say… they don't know." I was young and those I talked to kept telling me that I was too young to have those dreams and encounters, those powers that they didn't understand... YES, they did not know!

Here are the lyrics to Cathy Dennis' *Too Many Walls* which contain the message from my sister:

"Wish on a rainbow is all I can do

Dream of the good times that we never knew

No late nights in the warmth of your arms

I'll dream on

Living in wonder, thinking of you

Still looking for ways to uncover the truth

You're so young is all they can say

They don't know.

If I could change the way of the world

I'd be your girl

Too many walls have been built in between us

Too many dreams have been shattered around us

If I seem to give up they'll still never win

Deep in my heart I know the strength is within

Watching the others chances drift by

They'll never discover these feelings I hide

Deep inside I'm falling apart

All alone with a broken heart

Thinking in silence is all they allow
These words still unspoken may never be found
All these dreams one day will be mine
They cross my mind
My time has yet to come
Until then
Too many walls have been built in between us
Too many dreams have been shattered around us
If I seem to give up they'll still never win
Deep in my heart I know the strength is within."

I hope you all take my experience to heart and always remember: You're never too young or too old to really know the truth.

Chapter 14 – The Different Types of Hauntings

Before we take a look at some other encounters with ghosts I have experienced, I think it's important to describe the various types of hauntings. I have been a qualified paranormal investigator since 2007 and as part of my training, I had to learn about the differences in paranormal situations that people often encounter. The following explanations are not intended to be all encompassing, but I hope they will give you a better grasp of what constitutes a haunting.

The Residual Haunting

If we lived in a perfect world and you were able to choose the type of paranormal situation you would encounter, the residual haunting would probably be the best kind of haunting you could have. I can't honestly say for sure that a residual haunting necessarily contains an actual spirit.

In a residual haunting, an apparition appears in a structure at approximately the same time in each and every instance, and it does the very same thing every time it appears. Residual haunting spirits have no interaction with the living. In fact, if a person were to stand in the way of a residual haunting apparition, it would probably go right through that person as if they weren't there. Since they have no interaction with living persons, they are completely harmless; although they can be frightening and annoying.

Some residual haunting make no sense at all. I know of one instance where a home built in the 1700's was haunted on a residual basis. The house had undergone major renovations. This in itself could have contributed to the premises being haunted, because renovations can stir up spirits. The dining room had been converted into a living room and the kitchen had been expanded into the room that had once been the den.

Every night, the family who was now living in the house would see a woman dressed in the fashions of the 1700's. The female apparition would walk into the middle of the living room and serve food on what appeared to be a table. Since the dining room table was no longer in what was now the living room, her actions were completely out of place. It made no difference, though. The ghost would forever continue to place food on an imaginary table in what had once been the dining room, but no longer served that function.

Most paranormal investigators consider residual hauntings to be a case of energy being replayed over and over again, like a song on an MP3 player being set to repeat. They generally occur when a structure is located on or near a large amount of quartz. Quartz is a mineral that traps energy. It is used to power wrist watches, instead of batteries. The theory is that a residual haunting is a case of trapped energy being released and replayed for eternity. The quartz actually engulfed the energy taking place at that point in time, and released it at a specific time on a specific date to become a continuous engagement of an up close and personal "paranormal movie"

Intellectual Hauntings

These types of hauntings can be quite frightening. An intellectual haunting is one in which direct interaction takes place between a spirit and anyone in the vicinity of the spirit. The spirits involved are usually human spirits. Some are good natured and just want to establish some kind of communication, some are past family members and some can be downright angry and malicious.

These spirits will do many different things to attract attention. People have heard stomping noises, heard disembodied voices, experienced cold spots, witnessed objects being manipulated and encountered other paranormal phenomena. One theory about such spirits is that they are trapped in the time when they owned or occupied the house they are haunting; so they may not understand why new people are present. To them the house is still theirs.

Some intellectual hauntings occur by invitation. The spirits could have been summoned by a human or they could have entered the premises through an antique or other trinket that had been unwittingly brought into the place. All of the spirits I mention in this book are cases of intelligent hauntings, except for the haunting I encountered with the demon, which is a diabolical haunting.

Diabolical Hauntings

Diabolical hauntings are by far the most extreme forms of haunting known to mankind because they involve demons and other non-human evil entities. Demons are said to be fallen angels who sided with Lucifer, who is better known as the Devil. As a result, they were cast out of Heaven. These entities can use your worst fears, your most shocking secrets and other things against you, in order to force you to do what they want. They can be very persuasive, manipulative, and deceptive. In some cases they can even trick you by appearing as people or animals. This quality is known as being able to "shape shift"; and "shape shifters" actually do exist.

They can wreak havoc on your life and those around you. They like to invoke torment and to play with your mind and emotions. The worst part is that you cannot solve the problem by moving away from diabolical hauntings because these evil entities will follow; unlike the spirits in an intelligent haunting.

One good thing about demonic/diabolical haunting, though is that they are rare experiences. But when this kind of haunting occurs, you'll know it. The energy around you becomes so negative and thick that it you can almost hear it say: "Stay away!" Even if you are not psychic, you won't forget the feeling you get when if you are ever near a place occupied by a diabolical entity.

Chapter 15 – I Will Always See Ghosts

I have seen ghosts at all times of the day or night. I continue to see them whenever they have a need or desire to communicate with me, and I'm sure this will go on for the rest of my life.

The entities can appear as full body apparitions in my presence, or they might appear in my dreams. They may have something to say to me, or they may be warning me that something is going to happen or that someone is in need of my help.

The best time for them to contact me seems to be at night or at twilight time; which is between 11:00 P.M. and 2:00 A.M. This is because of the lunar energy.

The entities are not limited to only people. Fran and I had a dog named Buttons. We lost her at 2:00 A.M. on February 15th, 2009. I now see Buttons all the time. I see spirits while I am writing at night and working on my photography. I have two certified haunted dolls in my home that I used for a photo shoot. I see the spirits connected to those dolls all the time. I also frequently see my departed grandparents.

Most of the spirits I see are people who were close to me while they were in this world. They get in contact with me because they have messages to relate. Sometimes I see negative spirits, but they are people who were violent in life. An example of this was the one I encountered at the May-Stringer home in Brooksville, Florida. I have photographic evidence of where that nasty spirit pummeled me so hard on my chest that it left a handprint of some residue on my shirt and a scratch on my skin underneath. The negative spirit was not a demon, though. There has been only that one occasion when I ran into a diabolical nonhuman, otherwise known as a "demon", and that was nearly twenty years ago.

I'll be the first to admit that it is strange to see entities. This is why even to this day I tend not to shake hands with strangers or give hugs, and why I tend to avoid big groups and large events. I don't watch the news on TV and I can't be on the phone for too long because I can read energy from people and those scenarios drain me. I can't avoid feeling what people are feeling. After being on the phone all day, I am loaded with energy from other people… both positive and negative… and my own energy is zapped. If I happen to watch the news on TV and it carries a report of someone being executed, murdered or seriously injured, I empathize so strongly with subjects of the news stories that I see their last moments and know what is going through their heads. This is why news programs really bother me.

While I was growing up, I became reclusive because I didn't want others to see what I saw or to notice the spirits who were following me. I was worried that they would freak out. I didn't realize until I was older that they couldn't see them.

I regard the spirit of my unborn sister as an angel, but since she is my twin, I feel that she is part of me. Hurting me is also like hurting her. I'm sure she can feel it. There are times when I get really depressed without any apparent reason, and I believe that is because I'm feeling her pain, isolation and depression. She wants to be with me here in this world. Most twins feel that same sort of closeness, and I think she is trying to help me.

I also believe that the hardest part for her was me not knowing about her. That really got to her more than anything.

She appeared after I faced and overcame the demon. I still see her in my dreams, and there are also times when I physically see her in person.

I am very well protected because of my twin sister. I truly believe that my twin sister has something to do with the demon offering little resistance when I went toe to toe with it. Spirits do not dare hurt me or mess me when I venture into haunted places, all because of her. There have been more recent examples of how she has protected me, and not all of these instances involved the paranormal.

In 2009, Frances and I went to an old cemetery on Cemetery Road in Zephyrhills, Florida with two friends; Melissa and Megan. Megan and Melissa were classmates of mine at Land O'Lakes High, and we are all about the same age. Megan has spina bifida and she walked with crutch then. It was on Halloween Night, and this was a way to celebrate.

The cemetery was pretty old. It had the right atmosphere to be a haunting place. We had not been on any ghost hunts lately and I had heard about the old cemetery, so we decided to check it out. Megan and Melissa would go out on ghost hunts with Fran and me whenever they could. We would usually go to places where sightings had occurred. The right energy needs to be there.

There was an old sprawling house next door to the cemetery that seemed as though it had been a farm at one time. This wasn't at all surprising because Zephyrhills is a suburb of Tampa which originally consisted of farms. The old house was surrounded by some three acres of land. We heard some dogs barking, but there was a fence around the property, so everything seemed secure.

After we were at the cemetery for awhile, we saw a couple of orb-type things, but no ghosts. We didn't receive any negative vibrations, and there was no indication of anything being present that didn't want us around. All of a sudden, I saw something out of the corner of my eye that was moving by the fence. Then, I heard Megan say: "What's that?"

Suddenly, two dogs appeared. We had heard them barking off in the distance, but now they were right there in our midst, and they were growling and showing their fangs. One was a Doberman and the other was a Rottweiler. They both appeared ready to attack us. Even though there was a fence around their owner's house and surrounding property, the dogs had dug out a spot under the fence and had made it a large enough opening so that they could burrow down and squeeze under the fence to get into the cemetery.

Just as I turned to face the dogs, I saw them begin to charge Melissa. This caused me great concern not only for Melissa, but also for Megan, who was on a cane. I immediately darted to a place in between the dogs and Melissa.

Melissa was on the ground hollering: "JASON, THEY'LL HURT YOU!!" I told her: "Don't worry about it. Just get up and walk slowly away."

I tried to back the dogs up and turn them away by talking to them in an "I mean business" voice. I didn't cuss the dogs at all. I just hollered: "GET AWAY!! GET AWAY!!"

The dogs stepped back, but they tried to advance toward us a couple of more times. Each time, however, I was able to shoo them away with my voice and my commanding presence. It was clear to me that my twin sister was protecting me.

I finally noticed the hole that had enabled them to burrow under the fence, and I shooed them back in that direction. They went back to their yard. If the dogs had gotten close to Melissa, she would have been in trouble; and it would have been much worse for Megan, who had mobility issues. Both Megan and Melissa probably would have frozen from fear. One dog is bad enough, but handling two of them would have been nearly impossible.

As I mentioned before, I had another interesting experience in May-Stringer house in Brooksville, Florida that has become the Brooksville Heritage Museum. The house has been certified as haunted by The Atlantic Paranormal Society (TAPS). TAPS is a group featured on the SyFy channel's *Ghost Hunters* reality TV series. A sinister ghost named Mr. Nasty still lives in the attic of that house. The ghost is known to attack all females, as well as anyone who picks on it.

A reporter accompanied Frances and me into the attic of the historical house. We weren't in the attic long before I noticed a strong odor of something burning. I asked the docent who was with us about that pungent smell. She said: "We don't get it too often because there's nothing mechanical in the house. The burning smell comes when 'Mr. Nasty' is upset. Usually he just hits people."

Mr. Nasty took a swipe at me. The entity left me with a handprint on my shirt and a scratch on my chest. As I already mentioned, I have photographic evidence of both the handprint and the scratch. He didn't attack any more, and he left the women I was with alone. Once again my twin sister was watching over me.

These are only a couple of my more recent paranormal experiences. There will be many more to come, and I am not alone. More and more people are having encounters with ghosts, with entities and with demons. The paranormal is quite an intense subject. Its popularity has grown, and this has thrown up lots of controversy over whether or not there truly is life after death. This is a tough question not only for the established religions, but also for atheism. For if ghosts exist, there wouldn't be much basis for any atheistic theories which insist upon a scientific explanation for everything. There is one consolation, though. As opposed to the times of the Inquisition, there is little chance in today's western culture for anyone being hanged, tortured or burned at the stake for talking about it... LOL!

There is no need to bear hard feelings over the fact that there truly is some form of existence for all of us after our time on earth is over. Each and every community probably has ghosts, simply because each community has a history. The older a town is, the more likely it is that it will be haunted. Ghosts are part of our legacy, and we should support them by visiting haunted places. They are just like us in the sense that they don't want to spend their time all alone, either.

My Grandmother Visits Me from the Dead

In 1999 we received a call on Saturday from my aunt who informed us Ama was in the hospital and she wasn't doing well. She had been admitted to a hospital the day before after seeing a doctor for a routine checkup on her heart.

When we received the call on Saturday, she was already near death. Just a few hours later we received a call that she was gone. My grandfather tried to explain to me why they didn't call us sooner. I guess I understand.

Grandpa said "We were there thinking the worse, because she laid there looking like death warmed over. She wasn't moving, just sleeping. Then on Friday night, she woke up and Jason, OH HOW WONDERFUL SHE LOOKED! She had this glow about her, a glow I hadn't seen in years."

He added: "She ate dinner with me. We talked and laughed and the thought of losing her completely escaped my mind. Even the doctors said they were thinking she might be released as of Monday."

When Ama started to doze off that night, Grandpa kissed her goodbye and then headed out the door to go home for the night. He honestly thought she would be coming home soon. He had no idea that would be the last conversation and kiss he would ever share with her while she was still alive.

When he went to the hospital to see her on Saturday, he was shocked to see her lying quietly on the bed… too quiet. The doctors told him that she wasn't doing well; that she had taken a turn for the worse very late Friday night and was in coma. My grandfather immediately called everyone and told them to come to the hospital because Ama's time may have run out. My Uncle Mark decided to turn around and return to Connecticut. He had just left Connecticut a few hours before and was driving back to Ohio, so he wasn't far away.

In the middle of the afternoon, surrounded by my aunt, my Uncle Mark, my grandfather and my cousins, Ama took her last breath. My mom and I were not informed of this. We left that Sunday for Connecticut.

When I walked into my grandparents' home, things were so surreal. I went into the TV room and it wasn't the same. I saw an empty chair, with the book Ama had been reading on the table and her reading glasses on top of it. Her oxygen line was wrapped around the air tank. I used to use that oxygen line as a way of finding her. .

What really bothered me was that I wasn't there to say goodbye to her when she was still alive. The last time I had seen her alive was in 1998 when I brought Fran to Connecticut to introduce her to my grandparents.

Since Mom, my brother and I had no other place to stay; we spent the night at my grandparents' home. My brother slept in grandpa's bed, my mom in her old room and I slept in the playroom.

A few years before when my great aunt "Tantie" was placed in a nursing home, I asked that I be given her bed. It was the same bed my great grandmother passed away in, back in 1932. They had stored the bed in the playroom until I was able to pick it up. It was still there in 1999, so that was where I slept.

As I slept, I felt someone rubbing my leg and foot. It was a soft touching, gentle in nature and very warm. I woke up thinking: "It's probably Mom. She's sitting at the end of the bed because she's probably upset and couldn't sleep.

I opened my eyes to a startling sight. I sat up in my bed and hollered: "AMA!"

There she was, sitting at the end of my bed, rubbing my foot and leg like she used to do when I stayed over at her house. She looked so young and amazing, almost like the pictures I saw of her when my mom was young.

I said: "Ama, I thought you died! How can you be here? Am I dreaming?"

She replied: "Jason, dear dear Jason, I did die. I came back because I hadn't said goodbye to you. I couldn't leave without saying goodbye."

For the first time in a long while, a tear came to my eye. That almost never happened. But it was a tear of joy, rather than a tear of sorrow.

"Are you OK?" I asked her

"Yes, for the first time I am healthy. My heart is healed, I am not in pain... my energy is back and I feel so wonderful."

All I could do was smile. I knew how much pain she had been in. I saw her withering away before my very eyes; yet she never complained. I always admired her strength.

"Do you have to leave Ama," I said. "I know this is selfish, but please don't go I need you."

She smiled, walked over to my side and we both sat down on my bed. The bed actually dipped down from the weight of both of us. She said to me: "I wish I could, but remember I am always in your heart. Just look inside and I am right there. I have to go; because Heaven waits. But before I go, remember that I love you very much. Jesus loves you, and so do I. We will meet again in Heaven."

With that, she kissed my head, and I could actually feel her kiss like she was alive. She stood up and walked to the other side of the room. A blue glow began to form around her, and then she disappeared.

The next morning, my mother told me that Ama had appeared to her too. Mom described her just as I saw her.

At the funeral, I came face to face with my grandmother for the first time in over a year. She was in a light blue dress and she looked so peaceful in her casket. I wasn't upset or crying because I had seen her spirit the night before.

It has been my experience that most people do not look good in their caskets. This may account for why there are so many closed casket funerals. This was not the case with my grandmother; leave it to her to look her best even in death. She actually looked healthy! She was beautiful. She didn't have tubes hanging from her nose, and she wasn't bent over and riddled in pain. She was home with God!

Except for my mom, I took a lot of flak from my family, and they told me I acted in a very insensitive way. They thought I should have been acting more sorrowful. I never told them what happened to me the night before, so they had no idea of what was really going on.

All that mattered to me was that my grandmother was healthy and happy. It had torn me up inside to see her in pain.

Ironically, the last thing she said to me before I left Connecticut in 1998 was the very same thing she said to me before leaving my room that night… "Jesus loves you, and so do I. We will meet again in Heaven."

Back in 1996, I had asked her how she managed to deal with the pain. She said: "Jason, if you wear the Lord as your armor, you will get attacked and you will get some scratches, but you won't get mortally or severely injured." I live by those words to this very day, and that is how I cope with all the curve balls life throws at me.

What an amazing insight, and what an amazing woman! There isn't a day that goes by I don't miss Ama, and every now and then, I do see her in person.

A Kiss from the Grave

I finally returned to Connecticut in 2008. The last time I had been there was 1999 to bury my grandmother. When I attended her funeral, I had to leave early to get back in a hurry because of my job, so I never got to go back to the grave site the following day, when my family paid a visit. The first thing I wanted to do on my return in 2008 was visit Ama's grave.

Fran and I had a lot to do that day, so we got up early and traveled to Bristol, where West Cemetery is located. We found my grandmother's grave that morning. It was mid November, and it was very cold and wet. Instead of snow, it was freezing rain; and it was probably around 30 to 35 degrees outside. My grandmother was buried at the foot of a hill, and the grass was very green and slick.

I had brought along a photo of my grandmother sitting next to her last Christmas tree. I had taken that photo for her in 1998. It was my favorite memory of her, so I thought I would leave it at her gravesite. I had planned on digging a spot next to her head stone and burying it there. The only problem was that the ground was frozen solid.

I didn't want to just leave the photo at the grave. My family and I had had a falling out, and at that particular time, I didn't want to share the picture with them. I was planning to mend the animosity, but at the moment, I didn't know where that would lead or how it would go, and I didn't want to ruffle feathers. I wanted to leave the picture, but I didn't know where.

A few minutes went by, and then I got an amazing idea: I would lift Ama's foot stone and slide the photo under it. Nobody would know it was there and I would have accomplished my goal.

The idea of lifting the foot stone proved to be easier said than done. When I went to lift the stone, I thought: "Oh my god, is this heavy!" I hadn't realized how large the stone was. It took every ounce of strength that I had, but I finally got it up and out of the ground. I hollered out to Fran: "THROW THE FRIGGING PHOTO UNDER IT!!" My wife came through and she tossed it under the stone.

I dropped the stone and to my horror, it didn't go right back in the indentation it had made in the ground. I knew someone would see this and know that Ama's grave site had been tampered with. They might even trace the photo back to me. I panicked.

I started to jump on the stone and eventually it went back in the hole, but not perfectly. I am really obsessive compulsive with stuff like that, so I had to fix it.

The fix I came up with was to push the right side of the stone at its widest part. I moved over to that side of the stone, got down in a catcher's stance and placed my hand on the marble. My hands almost covered the entire length of that side.

I started to push with all my might, but it wasn't moving. Then, voila! It budged and as it did, my feet slipped on the icy wet slick grass. My back legs lifted into the air while my hands were still planted firm on the stone. I slipped forward fast. I could see my neck racing toward the jagged marble. If I had failed to avoid that catastrophe, I would have sliced my neck open and probably suffered the extreme irony of dying right on my grandmother's grave.

Then, as my chin hit the marble, I felt my shirt pull me back, and I regained my footing in the same catcher's stance I had started out in. I felt my chin in disbelief, only to determine that a chunk of my chin had been taken out right where my neck and bottom jaw met. It was bleeding.

I turned to Fran and thanked her for pulling me up. She said: "I didn't touch you. I actually saw your shirt pulled by something invisible. I'm amazed! I don't know what to say."

To this day, I still have the scar on my chin as a reminder of that incident. There is no doubt in my mind that Ama pulled me back and saved me from death. She was probably saying to herself: "OH, MY CLUMSY GRANDSON!!" She knew I was trying to do something special for her. My scar is my grandmother's permanent kiss, and I'll always be proud of it!

My Darling Orpha (1790-1972)

Late in 2011, I purchased two dolls that were certified as being haunted. I am very careful about obtaining such certification because, when I shoot a haunted object, I want it to be the genuine article. These dolls gave off EMF (Electro Magnetic Frequencies) wherever they were and they had a bit of a creepy feeling to them.

It is believed that when a spirit manifests itself, even if you cannot see it, it drains the energy from whatever is nearby and distorts the energy around it. This makes logical sense, since ghosts are a simple form of energy and anytime something interacts with itself… such as a ghost interacting with a cell phone tower… it would disburse or disturb energy.

EMF frequencies are usually found coming out of electrical outlets, circuit breaker boxes, high tension lines, as well as around computers and televisions. Other electrical equipment can give off EMF readings depending on how it is connected to a wall or whether something inside the unit is loose.

Whenever an investigation is undertaken, it is good practice for the investigator to perform a base EMF reading of the room in question. This should include checking all four corners of the room, looking up and down each wall and examining the center of the room. Once a base reading is determined, it is easy to find influxes and judge whether or not the influxes are standard to the room.

Getting back to my experience with the two dolls I purchased, I was photographing one of the creepy dolls around 1:00 A.M. From its appearance, there was no doubt it had been dug up from a grave. I happened to place the doll on a chair that had French words over it and I was using nothing but a tea light candle to provide lighting for the photo.

As I was photographing this doll the energy in the room became very stagnant. I knew something was going on.

As I was crouched down with the camera in front of my face, I turned and looked to the left side of the living room. Standing there was a female spirit who looked very upset. I think she may have thought I was hurting the doll. I saw the ghost start to lunge for me and as she did, my unborn twin sister popped up next to me. She wanted to protect me.

The spirit from the haunted doll ran into my sister and they disappeared into the night. As they vanished, a strong cool breeze blew my hair to one side.

Every now and then I see the spirits from the two haunted dolls, but they don't attack me anymore. In fact, I hear them talk to me all the time; especially late at night. It is actually quite soothing.

When my photo of the haunted doll was finished, I titled it: *My Darling Orpha (1790-1972)*. It is featured in the 3rd Volume of *Dreams, Nightmares, Fears and Fantasy.*

My Camera Takes Its Own Photograph

One peaceful afternoon I was sitting in an old cracker house in the Heritage Museum at Dade City, Florida. It was the first time I had ever been to the museum. I found it to be similar to Sturbridge Village in Sturbridge, Massachusetts, which was a place I would visit all the time when I was a kid.

Fran and I were going through this amazing yellow colored cracker house, and we paused in the parlor room to look at the furniture and tapestry which adorned that room. Suddenly, we heard a door open and close.

We both stepped back into the hallway, which was only one step away, and then we realized we were the only people in the entire house. The back door, which was nearest to Fran, was still closed, while the front door next to me was propped open. There were no other doors in the house.

I went to investigate and I noticed a pantry/storage door under the stairs that were located right at the entrance to the dining room. This door faced the back door; the one closest to Fran. I was relieved.

"It's just the wind blowing the door" I told Fran "Look, I'll open it and show you". Then as I went to open it, I realized the floor was warped next to the door, and that I couldn't move it easily. In fact, I really had to lean on it to get it open. When I went to close it, the door stopped about six inches from the door jam, which was where it hit the warped floor. When I pushed on the door, I heard another door slamming; and that slamming sound was very similar to first door slam we heard. It was so similar that I was 90% sure it was the same. There was no way the wind could have caused it. Whatever that had caused the door I was leaning on to slam… a door that had to clear a section of warped floor… would have to have been very strong indeed.

Fran wanted to leave, so we went out the back door into the separate kitchen. There was no door to that kitchen, just an open door frame.

I saw some amazing utensils in that old kitchen. I thought they would make a great still life photograph. So, I set up my camera on my tripod. I set the camera to take the picture by itself. I didn't want to use a flash because it would overexpose the picture, causing it to lose that "homey" effect.

I took a few steps away, and I was probably six feet from my camera so that I would be able to take in all the angles and make sure I got what I wanted when my camera took the picture automatically.

I saw the camera's LED screen pop on with a picture. I then immediately ran to the camera and took another picture. What I saw was amazing.

The first picture, the one taken by the camera itself, had a mist coming in from the left hand side of the photo. There was no visible mist visible to the human eye when the camera took the photo automatically. The photo also came out very bright, which was odd because the room was dark and no flash had occurred because none had been used.

There was a window on the right hand side, but all the light was coming from the left in the photo. There was a window on the left side of the kitchen, but the window was ten feet away from what was being photographed, and it barely illuminated the kitchen at all. In addition, the soffit protruded quite a distance off the wall, which meant that the window was covered from any outside light.

The second picture was strange, because it was dark with, no mist. I personally took it only seconds after the first picture was taken. It looked normal, almost the way I had envisioned it while I was setting up the shot.

That was enough for Fran, and we left the house. I can't say that we encountered a ghost, but it was a cool experience and it was definitely paranormal.

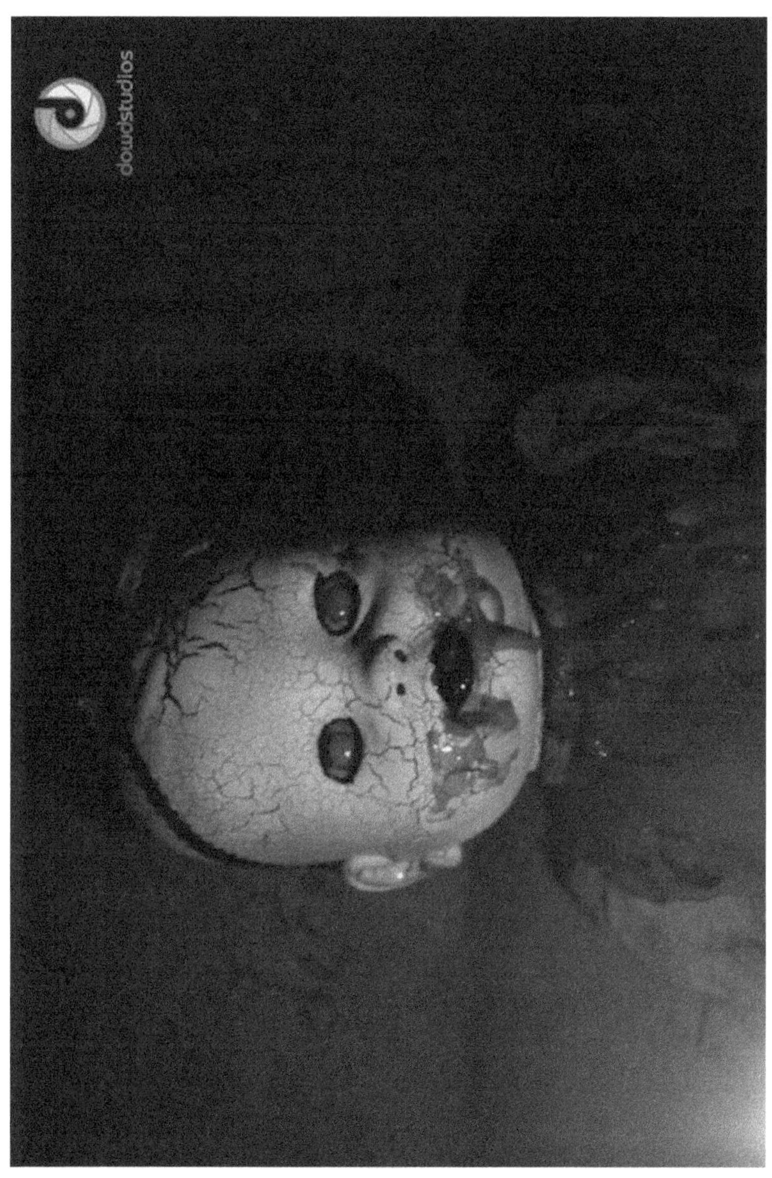

"My Darling Orpha 1790-1792"

Dreams, Nightmares, Fears and Fantasy Vol 3

www.ingramcontent.com/pod-product-compliance
Lightning Source LLC
Chambersburg PA
CBHW031207270326
41931CB00006B/449

* 9 7 8 0 6 1 5 6 2 8 7 3 8 *